DIVINE APPOINTMENTS

DAILY DEVOTIONALS BASED ON GOD'S CALENDAR: SUMMER

TRACY KRAUSS

Published by **Fictitious Ink Publishing**, Tumbler Ridge, BC, Canada, V0C 2W0

FOREWORD

Several years ago I began a journey which has profoundly changed my view of the world. I became fascinated with the Hebrew or Jewish calendar and started reading and researching. This expanded to daily prayer journaling about what I was learning. At some point the thought occurred to me that others might benefit from what God was teaching me. However, I am not a theologian. There are others more qualified to write such a book. Yet, I felt reassured to continue. This 'summer' edition is the second in a series, following the first book based on the 'spring' months of the year. It is not about a grand new revelation or any deep theological understanding on my part. It's a simple testament based on my own journey. It is my prayer that you will find something of value within these pages.

Tracy Krauss

INTRODUCTION

Why follow the Hebrew calendar?

Acts 17: 26

And He made from one, every nation of mankind to live on all the face of the earth, having determined their appointed times, and the boundaries of their habitation. (NASB)

In the Old Testament, God gave His people very specific instructions about the days of the week, months, and special feasts throughout the year. While many Jews continue to observe—or at least know about—this schedule of events, many Christians feel that following God's calendar is not relevant, or that the New Testament did away with these traditions. However, nowhere in scripture does it tell us to ignore the plans that God put in place. In fact, both Jesus and the early church followed the appointed times as laid out by God. One might argue that they did so because they were Jewish, but perhaps we need to be reminded that we have been 'grafted in' to that very tree! As a bonus, we are positioning ourselves for God's blessing when we align ourselves with His timing. It should be our desire to follow God's plan, not because we have to, but because it is a joy to do so. God is the one who set these timetables in motion, and He did not instruct us to change them. He is the same yesterday, today and forever.

This book walks readers through each season of the year by following the Hebrew months. Each day contains a short explanation or devotional, scripture to read and ponder, and a prayer focus. It is my attempt at introducing readers to the wonders of following God's calendar. I do not claim to be an expert, but only hope to offer what little insight God has given me as I strive to come closer to Him. May I suggest consulting a Jewish calendar in order to begin on the correct day.

The resources used are listed at the end of the book. References are general in that the idea to write down what I had been learning came well after the initial reading and research. When possible, I have given specific references, but most information was internalized and then regurgitated without having written specific quotations down.

Please remember that the point of observing God's calendar is *not* to take up a burden of tradition. We know that this is not necessary for our salvation. Instead, it is a way to celebrate and enhance our heritage as children of God. It is my prayer that as you follow along, you will be blessed beyond your own imagining.

1

TAMMUZ

T AMMUZ - Month 4
The Month of Reuben
29 days - June/July

THE FOURTH MONTH is the first of the three summer months which correspond with the tribes of Reuben, Simeon, and Gad. Unfortunately, when examining the history of Israel, a lot of tragic events occurred during the month of Tammuz. However, there is a redemptive side to the story. Even though Reuben fell into sin and had to pay the consequences, he didn't stay in his sin, but moved forward, displaying many redemptive qualities that are worth emulating. We, too, will fall into sin at times, but through Jesus, we can embrace the redemptive nature of God's love and leave our sinful past behind.

Tammuz Day 1 - Rosh Chodesh

As noted in the previous SPRING edition of this devotional series, the first day of each month is considered a special day called Rosh Chodesh, sometimes referred to as the 'new moon' in scripture. It is a day set aside to honour God by acknowledging the 'firstfruits' in our lives, including the first day of each month. (More on firstfruits in the SPRING edition of this series.)

As we celebrate this first day of a new month, think about the fact that we, as Christians, are a type of firstfruits. We are reborn as brand new creatures when we accept Christ as our Saviour. Dedicate this first day of Tammuz to Him and think about ways that you can shine His light into a dark and dying world. Also, consider tangible ways to honour Him with the firstfruits of your life. (For a possible list of 'firsts', refer to the first day of Nissan in the SPRING edition.)

Sᴄʀɪᴘᴛᴜʀᴇ:

James 1: 17 - 18

Every good thing given and every perfect gift is from above, coming down from the Father of lights, with whom there is no variation or shifting shadow. In the exercise of His will He brought us forth by the word of truth, so that we would be a kind of firstfruits among His creatures. (NASB)

Exoᴅᴜs 13: 2 and 12

Sanctify to Me every first-born, the first of offspring of

every womb among the sons of Israel, both of man and beast; it belongs to Me... That you shall devote to the Lord the first offspring of every womb, and the first offspring of every beast that you own; the males belong to the Lord. (NASB)

NUMBERS 3:12

Now behold, I have taken the Levites from among the sons of Israel instead of every firstborn, the first issue of the womb among the sons of Israel. So the Levites shall be mine. For the first-born are Mine; on the day that I struck down all the first-born in the land of Egypt, I sanctified to Myself all the first-born in Israel, from man to beast. They shall be Mine; I am the Lord. (NASB)

PRAYER FOCUS:

Help me to let my light shine for You this month, no matter what may come my way. Show me how I can honour You in specific and tangible ways with my first-fruits, not only today, but in the days, months, and years to come.

Tammuz Day 2

Each month of the Hebrew calendar corresponds with a letter of the alphabet, which in turn is found in Psalm 119, David's acrostic poem celebrating God's word. The month of Tammuz is represented by the letter CHET. (It may also be written as HHET and HETH)

Different sources have different meanings for this letter. It could indicate corralling something in—to fence in, stack stones around, or divide in half. God's word is like our safety zone. It provides boundaries which are for our own good. Another possible meaning of CHET has to do with livelihood. As we have seen previously, God's word is the source of everything we need. The final meaning for CHET is, 'light radiating from the eyes'. We've all heard the expression, "His eyes lit up!" What a wonderful picture of the joy of the Lord shining through us to others! The devil will try to put out our light, but we want our light to shine in the darkness, no matter our circumstances.

SCRIPTURE:

Psalm 119: 57 - 64
The Lord is my portion;
I have promised to keep Your words.
I sought Your favour with all my heart;
Be gracious to me according to Your word.
I considered my ways
And turned my feet to Your testimonies.
I hastened and did not delay
To keep Your commandments.
The cords of the wicked have encircled me,

But I have not forgotten Your law.
At midnight I shall rise to give thanks to You
Because of Your righteous ordinances.
I am a companion of all those who fear You,
And of those who keep Your precepts.
The earth is full of Your lovingkindness, Oh Lord;
Teach me Your statutes. (NASB)

PRAYER FOCUS:

Like the Psalmist, teach me Your ways, Oh Lord. You are my portion, my protection, and my guide. Your graciousness and lovingkindness knows no bounds. May I rise early to give thanks to You—even in the middle of the night if that's what You call me to do. Surround me with righteous companions—people who love Your Word, so that I may be a person of integrity and truth as I let the light of Your salvation radiate from my eyes.

Tammuz Day 3

During this month, we must continue to put into practice what God began in the first month, namely praising God first. The children of Israel started off strong, but soon became complacent and even fell into idolatry. It was during this month that they made and worshiped the golden calf. While we may think we would never fall away to such a degree, it is surprising how crafty the devil can be in drawing us away from intimacy with God, especially during the 'lazy days of summer'. Continue to follow Him in an attitude of worship, in order to avoid turning to idols —whatever that may mean to you on an individual basis, for idols can come in many forms.

SCRIPTURE:

Proverbs 4: 27

Do not swerve to the right or to the left; turn your foot away from evil. (ESV)

DEUTERONOMY 9:16

When I looked, I saw that you had sinned against the Lord your God; you had made for yourselves an idol cast in the shape of a calf. You had turned aside quickly from the way that the Lord had commanded you. (NIV)

Psalm 121

I will lift up my eyes to the mountains;
From where shall my help come?

My help comes from the Lord,
Who made heaven and earth.
He will not allow your foot to slip;
He who keeps you will not slumber.
Behold, He who keeps Israel
Will neither slumber nor sleep.
The Lord is your keeper;
The Lord is your shade on your right hand.
The sun will not smite you by day,
Nor the moon by night.
The Lord will protect you from all evil;
He will keep your soul.
The Lord will guard your going out
and your coming in
From this time forth and forever. (NASB)

PRAYER FOCUS:

Oh Lord, demolish all idols in my life, in the mighty name of Jesus! In self righteous smugness I might think I won't fall into idolatry, but the 'I-doll' is ever present, even luring believers to put themselves first above You. Reveal to me, and to Your church globally, where we need to change and cleanse our lives in order to get back on track with You. May I not become complacent or lazy in worshiping You, but help me to stay in an attitude and practice of worship, lest idolatry rise up.

Tammuz Day 4

The idea of light radiating from us to a dark world is a recurring theme this month. Isaiah prophesied about Zion that it would be radiant with the light of God's glory. May we shine that same light to a dying world.

Scripture:

Isaiah 60: 1 to 4a

Arise, shine, for your light has come, and the glory of the Lord rises upon you. See, darkness covers the earth and thick darkness is over the peoples, but the Lord rises upon you and His glory appears over you. Nations will come to your light, and kings to the brightness of your dawn. Lift up your eyes and look about you: All assemble and come to you; your sons come from afar, and your daughters are carried on the hip. Then you will look and be radiant, your heart will throb and swell with joy. (NIV)

Matthew 5: 16

In the same way, let your light shine before others, that they may see your good deeds and glorify your Father in heaven. (NIV)

Prayer focus:

Lord, show me how to be a light in a dark and dying world. May Your glory radiate from me as I live a life worthy of Your name. Help me to ever praise You, no matter my circumstances.

Tammuz Day 5

Ezekiel's vision of heaven took place on the fifth day of the fourth month. What a wonderful picture of the glory of the Lord!

SCRIPTURE:

Ezekiel 1

In my thirtieth year, in the fourth month on the fifth day, while I was among the exiles by the Kebar River, the heavens were opened and I saw visions of God.

On the fifth of the month - it was the fifth year of the exile of King Jehoiachin - the word of the Lord came to Ezekiel the priest, the son of Buzi, by the Kebar River in the land of the Babylonians. There the hand of the Lord was on him.

I looked, and I saw a windstorm coming out of the north - an immense cloud with flashing lightning and surrounded by brilliant light. The centre of the fire looked like glowing metal, and in the fire was what looked like four living creatures. In appearance their form was human, but each of them had four faces and four wings. Their legs were straight; their feet were like those of a calf and gleamed like burnished bronze. Under their wings on their four sides they had human hands. All four of them had faces and wings, and the wings of one touched the wings of another. Each one went straight ahead; they did not turn as they moved.

Their faces looked like this: Each of the four had the face of a human being, and on the right side each had the face of a lion, and on the left the face of an ox; each also had the face of an eagle. Such were their faces. They each had two wings spreading out upward, each wing touching that of the creature on either side; and each had two other wings covering its body. Each one went straight ahead. Wherever the spirit would go, they would go, without turning as they went. The appearance of the living creatures was like burning coals of fire or like torches. Fire moved back and forth among the creatures; it was bright, and lightning flashed out of it. The creatures sped back and forth like flashes of lightning.

As I looked at the living creatures, I saw a wheel on the ground beside each creature with its four faces. This was the appearance and structure of the wheels: They sparkled like topaz, and all four looked alike. Each appeared to be made like a wheel intersecting a wheel. As they moved, they would go in any one of the four directions the creatures faced; the wheels did not change direction as the creatures went. Their rims were high and awesome, and all four rims were full of eyes all around.

When the living creatures moved, the wheels beside them moved; and when the living creatures rose from the ground, the wheels also rose. Wherever the spirit would go, they would go, and the wheels would rise along with them, because the spirit of the living creatures was in the wheels. When the creatures moved, they also moved; when the creatures stood still, they also stood still; and when the creatures rose from the ground, the wheels rose along with them, because the spirit of the living creatures was in the wheels.

Spread out above the heads of the living creatures was what looked something like a vault, sparkling like crystal, and awesome. Under the vault their wings were stretched out one toward the other, and each had two wings covering its body. When the creatures moved, I heard the sound of their wings, like the roar of rushing waters, like the voice of the Almighty, like the tumult of an army. When they stood still, they lowered their wings.

Then there came a voice from above the vault over their heads as they stood with lowered wings. Above the vault over their heads was what looked like a throne of lapis lazuli, and high above on the throne was a figure like that of a man. I saw that from what appeared to be His waist up He looked like glowing metal, as if full of fire, and that from there down He looked like fire; and brilliant light surrounded him. Like the appearance of a rainbow in the clouds on a rainy day, so was the radiance around him.

This was the appearance of the likeness of the glory of the Lord. When I saw it, I fell facedown, and I heard the voice of one speaking. (NIV)

PRAYER FOCUS:

Open my eyes to the glory of Your holiness! As I worship You this month, may the heavens be opened to Your majesty so that I may serve You better.

Tammuz Day 6

Continuing with Ezekiel's vision, we too, are given a commission from the Lord which we must obey. In Matthew, the 'great commission' tells us to go and preach the good news to everyone.

SCRIPTURE:

Ezekiel 2

He said to me, "Son of man stand up on your feet and I will speak to you." As He spoke, the Spirit came into me and raised me to my feet, and I heard Him speaking to me.

He said: "Son of man, I am sending you to the Israelites, to a rebellious nation that has rebelled against me; they and their ancestors have been in revolt against me to this very day. The people to whom I am sending you are obstinate and stubborn. Say to them, 'This is what the Sovereign Lord says.' And whether they listen or fail to listen - for they are a rebellious people - they will know that a prophet has been among them. And you, son of man, do not be afraid of them or their words. Do not be afraid, though briers and thorns are all around you and you live among scorpions. Do not be afraid of what they say or be terrified by them, though they are a rebellious people. You must speak my words to them, whether they listen or fail to listen, for they are rebellious. But you, son of man, listen to what I say to you. Do not rebel like that rebellious people; open your mouth and eat what I give you."

Then I looked, and I saw a hand stretched out to me. In

it was a scroll, which He unrolled before me. On both sides of it were written words of lament and mourning and woe. (NIV)

Ezekiel 3: 17 - 19

Son of man, I have made you a watchman for the people of Israel; so hear the word I speak and give them warning from me. When I say to a wicked person, 'You will surely die,' and you do not warn them or speak out to dissuade them from their evil ways in order to save their life, that wicked person will die for their sin, and I will hold you accountable for their blood. But if you do warn the wicked person and they do not turn from their wickedness or from their evil ways, they will die for their sin; but you will have saved yourself. (NIV)

Matthew 28: 18 - 20

Then Jesus came to them and said, "All authority in heaven and on earth has been given to me. Therefore go and make disciples of all nations, baptizing them in the name of the Father and of the Son and of the Holy Spirit, and teaching them to obey everything I have commanded you. And surely I am with you always, to the very end of the age." (NIV)

Prayer focus:

Lord, give me the courage to go where You want me to

go and to speak what You want me to speak. You have made each believer a 'watchman', as Ezekiel was, and it is up to us to obey. Your command to all believers is to go and make disciples of all nations. Help me to obey that command.

Tammuz Day 7

Ezekiel's vision mirrors that of John's in Revelation. Again, we see the majesty and holiness of the Sovereign Lord, who is worthy of all our praise.

SCRIPTURE:

Revelation 1: 12 - 18

I turned around to see the voice that was speaking to me. And when I turned I saw seven golden lampstands, and among the lampstands was someone like a son of man, dressed in a robe reaching down to His feet and with a golden sash around His chest. The hair on His head was white like wool, as white as snow, and His eyes were like blazing fire. His feet were like bronze glowing in a furnace, and His voice was like the sound of rushing waters. In His right hand He held seven stars, and coming out of His mouth was a sharp, double-edged sword. His face was like the sun shining in all its brilliance.

When I saw Him, I fell at His feet as though dead. Then He placed His right hand on me and said: "Do not be afraid. I am the First and the Last. I am the Living One; I was dead, and now look, I am alive for ever and ever! And I hold the keys of death and Hades. (NIV)

REVELATION 4: 2 - 11

At once I was in the Spirit, and there before me was a throne in heaven with someone sitting on it. And the one who sat there had the appearance of jasper and ruby. A rainbow that shone like an emerald encircled the throne. Surrounding the throne were twenty-four other thrones, and seated on them were twenty-four elders. They were dressed in white and had crowns of gold on their heads. From the throne came flashes of lightning, rumblings and peals of thunder. In front of the throne, seven lamps were blazing. These are the seven spirits of God. Also in front of the throne there was what looked like a sea of glass, clear as crystal.

In the centre, around the throne, were four living creatures, and they were covered with eyes, in front and in back. The first living creature was like a lion, the second was like an ox, the third had a face like a man, the fourth was like a flying eagle. Each of the four living creatures had six wings and was covered with eyes all around, even under its wings. Day and night they never stop saying, "Holy, holy, holy is the Lord God Almighty, who was, and is, and is to come."

Whenever the living creatures give glory, honour and thanks to Him who sits on the throne and who lives for ever and ever, the twenty-four elders fall down before Him who sits on the throne and worship Him who lives for ever and ever. They lay their crowns before the throne and say, "You are worthy, our Lord and God, to receive glory and honour and power, for You created all things, and by Your will they were created and have their being." (NIV)

PRAYER FOCUS:
You are worthy of praise and honour today, oh Lord

God. With the living creatures and the elders I cry, "Holy, holy, holy are You Lord! You are worthy to receive all glory and honour and power!" Hallelujah!

Tammuz Day 8

The visions experienced by Ezekiel and John were life changing. But guess what? God hasn't changed! If we can catch a vision of who God truly is, in all His holiness and splendour, it will change the way we view the world. May our eyes 'light up' with the glory of His majesty!

SCRIPTURE:

Hebrews 1: 1 - 12

In the past God spoke to our ancestors through the prophets at many times and in various ways, but in these last days He has spoken to us by His Son, whom He appointed heir of all things, and through whom also He made the universe. The Son is the radiance of God's glory and the exact representation of His being, sustaining all things by His powerful word. After He had provided purification for sins, He sat down at the right hand of the Majesty in heaven. So He became as much superior to the angels as the name He has inherited is superior to theirs.

For to which of the angels did God ever say, "You are my Son; today I have become your Father"? Or again, "I will be His Father, and He will be my Son"?

And again, when God brings His firstborn into the world, He says, "Let all God's angels worship Him."

In speaking of the angels He says, "He makes His angels spirits, and His servants flames of fire." But about the Son He says, "Your throne, O God, will last for ever and ever; a sceptre of justice will be the sceptre of Your kingdom. You have loved righteousness and hated wickedness; therefore God, Your God, has set You above Your companions by anointing You with the oil of joy."

He also says, "In the beginning, Lord, You laid the foundations of the earth, and the heavens are the work of Your hands. They will perish, but You remain; they will all wear out like a garment. You will roll them up like a robe; like a garment they will be changed. But You remain the same, and Your years will never end." (NIV)

PRAYER FOCUS:

Lord, reveal Yourself in Your glory and splendour. The same resurrection power that was evident in Ezekiel's vision is still at work in believers today. Show me Your glory that I might fully know You.

Tammuz Day 9

As we continue to move forward this year, we must remember that worshiping the Lord should be our first priority. Only then will everything else fall into place. We are called to worship the Lord in spirit and in truth—even in difficult circumstances.

SCRIPTURE:

Joshua 24: 14 and 15

Now, therefore, fear the Lord and serve Him in sincerity and truth; and put away the gods which your fathers served beyond the river and in Egypt, and serve the Lord. If it is disagreeable in your sight to serve the Lord, choose for yourselves today whom you will serve: whether the gods which your fathers served which were beyond the River, or the gods of the Amorites in whose land you are living; but as for me and my house, we will serve the Lord." (NASB)

JOB 1: 20 - 22

Then Job arose and tore his robe and shaved his head and fell on the ground and worshiped. And he said, "Naked I came from my mother's womb, and naked shall I return. The Lord gave, and the Lord has taken away; blessed be the name of the Lord." In all this Job did not sin or charge God with wrong.

(ESV)

.   .   .

Psalm 30

I will extol You, Oh Lord, for You have drawn me up
and have not let my foes rejoice over me.
Oh Lord my God, I cried to You for help,
and You have healed me.
Oh Lord, You have brought up my soul from Sheol;
You restored me to life from among those
who go down to the pit.
Sing praises to the Lord, oh you His saints,
and give thanks to His holy name.
For His anger is but for a moment,
and His favour is for a lifetime.
Weeping may tarry for the night,
but joy comes with the morning.
As for me, I said in my prosperity,
"I shall never be moved."
By Your favour, oh Lord,
You made my mountain stand strong;
You hid Your face; I was dismayed.
To You, oh Lord, I cry,
and to the Lord I plead for mercy:
What profit is there in my death,
if I go down to the pit?
Will the dust praise You?
Will it tell of Your faithfulness?
Hear, oh Lord, and be merciful to me!
Oh Lord, be my helper!"
You have turned for me my mourning into dancing;
You have loosed my sackcloth
and clothed me with gladness,
that my glory may sing Your praise and not be silent.

Oh Lord my God, I will give thanks to You forever!
(ESV)

PRAYER FOCUS:

Worshipping You and following Your ways is a choice.
Help me be like Joshua when he declared that He would
serve You along with his entire household. I lift up the
members of my family—even those who do not know You
or who are not serving You, and declare that they will
come into alignment with Your purposes and plan. Like
Job, help me to weather whatever circumstances come my
way, always praising and thanking You in every situation.
You can turn mourning into dancing, and I praise Your
holy name today.

Tammuz Day 10

We know that the enemy of our souls would like nothing better than to see us turn away from God, and therefore, he attacks us whenever he can. Thankfully, God has provided us with a means of protection. We are told to put on the whole armour of God, including the breastplate of righteousness.

Scripture:

Isaiah 59: 17

And He put on righteousness like a breastplate, and a helmet of salvation on His head; and He put on garments of vengeance for clothing, and wrapped Himself with zeal as a mantle. (NASB)

Ephesians 6: 10 - 17

Finally, be strong in the Lord and in His mighty power. Put on the full armour of God, so that you can take your stand against the devil's schemes. For our struggle is not against flesh and blood, but against the rulers, against the authorities, against the powers of this dark world and against the spiritual forces of evil in the heavenly realms. Therefore put on the full armour of God, so that when the day of evil comes, you may be able to stand your ground, and after you have done everything, to stand. Stand firm then, with the belt of truth buckled around your waist, with the breastplate of righteousness in place, and with your feet fitted with the readiness that comes from the gospel of peace. In addition to all this, take up the shield of faith, with which you can extinguish all the flaming arrows of the evil one. Take the helmet of salvation and the sword of the Spirit, which is the word of God. (NIV)

2 CORINTHIANS 2: 10 - 11

But one whom you forgive anything, I forgive also; for indeed what I have forgiven, if I have forgiven anything, I did it for your sakes in the presence of Christ, so that no advantage would be taken of us by Satan, for we are not ignorant of his schemes. (NASB)

PRAYER FOCUS:

I pray for divine insight into the devil's schemes so that he may never attack me or my loved ones unawares. I continue to worship You today, Oh Lord God, and pray that You would show me how to secure the breastplate of righteousness over my heart, while also fitting the rest of the armour in place. Show me those whom I need to forgive and those whom I have offended, so that no scheme of the enemy would prosper against me or my household.

Tammuz Day 11

As we already discovered, Tammuz is the month of Reuben. He was the firstborn, but lost his claim by disgracing his father Jacob when he slept with his concubine, Bilhah. Even though Reuben had to suffer the consequences of his sin, he did receive a blessing from his father. In fact, there are a lot of tragic events in Israel's history that occur during this month, but there is a redemptive side, too, as we shall see.

Scripture:

Genesis 35: 22

While Israel was living in that region, Reuben went in and slept with his father's concubine Bilhah, and Israel heard of it.

(NIV)

Genesis 49: 1 - 4

Then Jacob called his sons and said, "Gather yourselves together, that I may tell you what shall happen to you in days to come. Assemble and listen, O sons of Jacob, listen to Israel your father. Reuben, you are my firstborn, my might, and the firstfruits of my strength, preeminent in dignity and preeminent in power. Unstable as water, you shall not have preeminence, because you went up to your father's bed; then you defiled it - he went up to my couch!

(ESV)

. . .

Isaiah 12: 1 and 2

Then you will say on that day, "I will give thanks to Thee, oh Lord; for although Thou wast angry with me, thine anger is turned away, and thou dost comfort me. Behold, God is my salvation. I will trust and not be afraid; for the Lord God is my strength and song, and He has become my salvation." (NASB)

Prayer focus:

I come before You today, Lord, recognizing my own sinful nature and the fact that no one—not even one—is blameless. However, I thank You today that You have provided a way for all to be washed clean, and that Your redemption is able to take away all sin and make us new. Forgive me for my sin, both those that I know about, and those that I don't know or remember. I pray for a restoration of Your might, power and strength, through the first-born son of the resurrection, Jesus Christ.

Tammuz Day 12

The literal meaning of the name Reuben is "Behold a son!" He was Jacob's firstborn, and Leah took his birth to be a sign of favour from God. After all, we know from scripture that Jacob didn't love Leah and had been tricked into marrying her. However, in Genesis 29:32 she says, "The Lord has surely looked on my affliction. Now therefore, my husband will love me." Leah is often seen as a pathetic character, and we feel sorry for her because her husband didn't love her, but God had a purpose for her life. She bore six of the twelve tribes, including the forefather of the Messiah, as well as Dinah, the only daughter mentioned.

Scripture:

Jeremiah 31: 13

Then young women will dance and be glad, young men and old as well. I will turn their mourning into gladness; I will give them comfort and joy instead of sorrow. (NIV)

Genesis 35: 23

The sons of Leah: Reuben the firstborn of Jacob, Simeon, Levi, Judah, Issachar and Zebulun. (NIV)

Isaiah 12: 3 - 6

Therefore you will joyously draw water from the springs of salvation. And in that day you will say, "Give thanks to the Lord. Call on His name. Make known His deeds among the people; make them remember that His name is exalted." Praise the Lord in song, for He has done excellent things; let this be known throughout the earth. Cry aloud and shout for joy, oh inhabitants of Zion, for great in your midst is the Holy One of Israel. (NASB)

PRAYER FOCUS:

Show me how to be in alignment with Your plan for my life, no matter the circumstances. May I ever look to You and trust that You know the greater good, no matter what I am going through. Teach me how to rejoice in You always.

Tammuz Day 13

Reuben is mentioned again in Genesis 30 when he found mandrakes in the field and took them to his mother. Mandrakes were thought to be an aid for infertility and were also considered an aphrodisiac. Whether he found the mandrakes of his own volition, or whether he was instructed to do so by his mother, we are not told. However, the mandrakes were used to strike a deal between Leah and Rachel. The rivalry for their husband's affection had continued for many years between the two sisters, and in this case, Leah gave Rachel the mandrakes in exchange for the privilege of sleeping with Jacob. Although this certainly doesn't align with a modern sense of morality, it does demonstrate Reuben's obedience and a willingness to assist his family in keeping the peace. It also shows a certain tenacity on Leah's part in claiming her rights as Jacob's wife.

SCRIPTURE:

Genesis 30: 14 - 16

In the days of wheat harvest Reuben went and found mandrakes in the field and brought them to his mother Leah. Then Rachel said to Leah, "Please give me some of your son's mandrakes." But she said to her, "Is it a small matter that you have taken away my husband? Would you take away my son's mandrakes also?" Rachel said, "Then he may lie with you tonight in exchange for your son's mandrakes." When Jacob came from the field in the evening, Leah went out to meet him and said, "You must come in to me, for I have hired you with my son's mandrakes." So he lay with her that night. (ESV)

SONG OF SOLOMON 7: 11 - 13

Come, my beloved, let us go out into the fields and lodge in the villages; let us go out early to the vineyards and see whether the vines have budded, the grape blossoms have opened and the pomegranates are in bloom. There I will give you my love. The mandrakes give forth fragrance, and beside our doors are all choice fruits, new as well as old, which I have laid up for you, O my beloved. (ESV)

PRAYER FOCUS:

I pray for Your blessing over me, Lord, and claim my rights as Your bride. I love You and worship You today, and pray that the fragrance of Your Holy Spirit would waft over me like perfume.

Tammuz Day 14

Reuben showed love and compassion when the other brothers wanted to kill Joseph. Reuben was the one who convinced them to put Joseph in a pit instead of killing him, intending to rescue him later. This is interesting because Reuben had as much reason to hate Joseph as the rest of his brothers— perhaps even more! He was the first-born and should have received all of his father's honour, but instead his birthright went to Joseph, Jacob's favoured son. Still, Reuben knew that Joseph's death would be devastating to his father, and he wanted to honour his elder above his own feelings.

SCRIPTURE:

Genesis 37: 17 - 22

And the man said, "They have gone away, for I heard them say, 'Let us go to Dothan.'" So Joseph went after his brothers and found them at Dothan. They saw him from afar, and before he came near to them they conspired against him to kill him. They said to one another, "Here comes this dreamer. Come now, let us kill him and throw him into one of the pits. Then we will say that a fierce animal has devoured him, and we will see what will become of his dreams." But when Reuben heard it, he rescued him out of their hands, saying, "Let us not take his life." And Reuben said to them, "Shed no blood; throw him into this pit here in the wilderness, but do not lay a hand on him" - that he might rescue him out of their hand to restore him to his father. (ESV)

· · ·

1 CHRONICLES 5: 1

Now the sons of Reuben the firstborn of Israel (for he was the firstborn, but because he defiled his father's bed, his birthright was given to the sons of Joseph the son of Israel; so that he is not enrolled in the genealogy according to birthright.) (NASB)

LAMENTATIONS 3: 22 - 33

Because of the Lord's great love we are not consumed,
for His compassions never fail.
They are new every morning;
great is Your faithfulness.
I say to myself, "The Lord is my portion;
therefore I will wait for Him."
The Lord is good to those whose hope is in Him,
to the one who seeks Him;
it is good to wait quietly for the salvation of the Lord.
It is good for a man to bear the yoke while he is young.
Let him sit alone in silence,
for the Lord has laid it on him.
Let him bury his face in the dust -
there may yet be hope.
Let him offer his cheek to one who would strike him,
and let him be filled with disgrace.
For no one is cast off by the Lord forever.
Though He brings grief, He will show compassion,
so great is His unfailing love.
For He does not willingly bring affliction
or grief to anyone. (NIV)

. . .

MATTHEW 5: 38 - 42

You have heard that it was said, 'Eye for eye, and tooth for tooth.' But I tell you, do not resist an evil person. If anyone slaps you on the right cheek, turn to them the other cheek also. And if anyone wants to sue you and take your shirt, hand over your coat as well. If anyone forces you to go one mile, go with them two miles. Give to the one who asks you, and do not turn away from the one who wants to borrow from you. (NIV)

PRAYER FOCUS:

Lord, I pray that You would remove envy from my life. Forgive me for the times I have grumbled and complained about my lot in life, especially in comparison to others. Help me to be upright in heart in everything I do, always putting others ahead of myself.

Tammuz Day 15

While in Egypt, Reuben offers the lives of his own two sons in Benjamin's place should anything happen to him, the youngest brother. Even though Reuben lost the right of the firstborn because of his sin, he pulled himself up and moved forward, acting with integrity and leadership like a natural firstborn should do. He is an example of a man who had to live with the consequences of his sin, but showed true repentance as he moved forward.

Scripture:

Genesis 42: 21 - 38

They said to one another, "Surely we are being punished because of our brother. We saw how distressed he was when he pleaded with us for his life, but we would not listen; that's why this distress has come on us."

Reuben replied, "Didn't I tell you not to sin against the boy? But you wouldn't listen! Now we must give an accounting for his blood." They did not realize that Joseph could understand them, since he was using an interpreter.

He turned away from them and began to weep, but then came back and spoke to them again. He had Simeon taken from them and bound before their eyes.

Joseph gave orders to fill their bags with grain, to put each man's silver back in his sack, and to give them provisions for their journey. After this was done for them, they loaded their grain on their donkeys and left.

At the place where they stopped for the night one of them opened his sack to get feed for his donkey, and he saw his silver in the mouth of his sack. "My silver has been returned," he said to his brothers. "Here it is in my sack."

Their hearts sank and they turned to each other trembling and said, "What is this that God has done to us?"

When they came to their father Jacob in the land of Canaan, they told him all that had happened to them. They said, "The man who is lord over the land spoke harshly to us and treated us as though we were spying on the land. But we said to him, 'We are honest men; we are not spies. We were twelve brothers, sons of one father. One is no more, and the youngest is now with our father in Canaan.'

"Then the man who is lord over the land said to us, 'This is how I will know whether you are honest men: Leave one of your brothers here with me, and take food for your starving households and go. But bring your youngest brother to me so I will know that you are not spies but honest men. Then I will give your brother back to you, and you can trade in the land.' "

As they were emptying their sacks, there in each man's sack was his pouch of silver! When they and their father saw the money pouches, they were frightened. Their father Jacob said to them, "You have deprived me of my children. Joseph is no more and Simeon is no more, and now you want to take Benjamin. Everything is against me!"

Then Reuben said to his father, "You may put both of my sons to death if I do not bring him back to you. Entrust him to my care, and I will bring him back."

But Jacob said, "My son will not go down there with you; his brother is dead and he is the only one left. If harm comes to him on the journey you are taking, you will bring my gray head down to the grave in sorrow." (NIV)

PRAYER FOCUS:

I pray that You would help me to be a person of integrity in everything that I do. Empower me by Your Holy Spirit to stand up for righteousness and to take on a mantle of leadership for Your kingdom and Your glory.

Tammuz Day 16

Reuben learned from his mistakes and demonstrates for us the fruit of repentance. When Moses blessed the tribes before his death, he imparted a redemptive blessing upon the tribe of Reuben, although they still had to pay the consequences for their sins.

Scripture:

Deuteronomy 33: 6 (Moses blessing)
"Let Reuben live, and not die, but let his men be few." (ESV)

Romans 6: 14

For sin shall not be master over you, for you are not under law, but under grace. (NASB)

Hebrews 9: 15

Therefore He is the mediator of a new covenant, so that those who are called may receive the promised eternal inheritance, since a death has occurred that redeems them from the transgressions committed under the first covenant. (ESV)

Prayer Focus:

Thank you for the power of Your redemption and the new covenant that all believers have with You. Help me to move past my mistakes and to focus on serving You.

Tammuz Day 17

On the seventeenth day of Tammuz, the people of Israel sinned while in the wilderness by making a golden calf and bowing down to it. Later in their history, this day was the beginning of a three week period of destruction ending on the ninth day of Av (the fifth month) in which the temple was destroyed in Jerusalem. In Jewish tradition, this is a sober time of reflection to make sure that one does not turn aside from the Lord lest disaster strike. While we are not bound by superstitions, it is prudent to spend some time in sober reflection as we examine our own lives to make sure we have not allowed any idols to infiltrate and turn us away from worshiping the one true God.

Scripture:

Exodus 32: 4 - 8

And he received the gold from their hand and fashioned it with a graving tool and made a golden calf. And they said, "These are your gods, O Israel, who brought you up out of the land of Egypt!" When Aaron saw this, he built an altar before it. And Aaron made a proclamation and said, "Tomorrow shall be a feast to the Lord." And they rose up early the next day and offered burnt offerings and brought peace offerings. And the people sat down to eat and drink and rose up to play.

And the Lord said to Moses, "Go down, for your people, whom you brought up out of the land of Egypt, have corrupted themselves. They have turned aside quickly out of the way that I commanded them. They have made for themselves a golden calf and have worshiped it and sacrificed to it and said, 'These are your gods, O Israel, who brought you up out of the land of Egypt!'" And the Lord said to Moses, "I have seen this people, and behold, it is a stiff-necked people. Now therefore let me alone, that my wrath may burn hot against them and I may consume them, in order that I may make a great nation of you."

But Moses implored the Lord his God and said, "O Lord, why does Your wrath burn hot against Your people, whom you have brought out of the land of Egypt with great power and with a mighty hand? Why should the Egyptians say, 'With evil intent did He bring them out, to kill them in the mountains and to consume them from the face of the earth'? Turn from Your burning anger and relent from this disaster against Your people. Remember Abraham, Isaac, and Israel, Your servants, to whom You swore by Your own self, and said to them, 'I will multiply your offspring as the stars of heaven, and all this land that I have promised I will give to your offspring, and they shall inherit it forever.'" And the Lord relented from the disaster that He had spoken of bringing on His people. (ESV)

PRAYER FOCUS:

Keep me from idols, Oh Lord! I will not fall for any 'golden calf' that may be presented. Make me like Moses —a person who followed You without wavering and who entreated Your mercy on behalf of others. Reveal to me any idols of my own making, so that I might purge from my life anything that would exalt itself over You.

Tammuz Day 18

The tribe of Reuben was paired with Simeon and Gad for camping and marching. They camped to the south of the tabernacle and marched out second after the first group, which was comprised of Judah, Issachar and Zebulun. Reuben's group had the second largest number of warriors, second only to the first group already mentioned. This would have been important should the Israelites come under attack. They would have the versatility to assist with the battle in front, or move to the back and help the rearguard. Also, they were next to the Levites, who were in charge of the tabernacle and all of the holy objects. This fierce group of warriors would have ensured that God's Most Holy things were kept safe from harm.

Scripture:

Numbers 2: 10 - 17

On the south side shall be the standard of the camp of Reuben by their companies, the chief of the people of Reuben being Elizur the son of Shedeur, his company as listed being 46,500. And those to camp next to him shall be the tribe of Simeon, the chief of the people of Simeon being Shelumiel the son of Zurishaddai, his company as listed being 59,300. Then the tribe of Gad, the chief of the people of Gad being Eliasaph the son of Reuel, his company as listed being 45,650. All those listed of the camp of Reuben, by their companies, were 151,450. They shall set out second. Then the tent of meeting shall set out, with the camp of the Levites in the midst of the camps; as they camp, so shall they set out, each in position, standard by standard. (ESV)

PRAYER FOCUS:

   I pray that You would enable me to be versatile for You, going where You call me to go, and battling in whatever capacity You deem necessary. May I always be ready for the call, whether behind or before, fitted with the armour of God, and ready to defend Your honour.

Tammuz Day 19

When they received their inheritance, the tribe of
Reuben, along with Gad and half of Manassah, chose to
take their inheritance on the east side of the Jordan River.
However, they were faithful to go to war with the rest of
the tribes to secure the entire inheritance for everyone.

SCRIPTURE:

Numbers 32: 1 - 7; and 16 - 25

Now the people of Reuben and the people of Gad had
a very great number of livestock. And they saw the land of
Jazer and the land of Gilead, and behold, the place was a
place for livestock. So the people of Gad and the people of
Reuben came and said to Moses and to Eleazar the priest
and to the chiefs of the congregation, "Ataroth, Dibon,
Jazer, Nimrah, Heshbon, Elealeh, Sebam, Nebo, and Beon,
the land that the Lord struck down before the congregation of Israel, is a land for livestock, and your servants have
livestock." And they said, "If we have found favour in your
sight, let this land be given to your servants for a possession. Do not take us across the Jordan."

But Moses said to the people of Gad and to the people
of Reuben, "Shall your brothers go to the war while you sit
here? Why will you discourage the heart of the people of
Israel from going over into the land that the Lord has given
them?"...

Then they came near to him and said, "We will build
sheepfolds here for our livestock, and cities for our little
ones, but we will take up arms, ready to go before the
people of Israel, until we have brought them to their place.

And our little ones shall live in the fortified cities because of the inhabitants of the land. We will not return to our homes until each of the people of Israel has gained his inheritance. For we will not inherit with them on the other side of the Jordan and beyond, because our inheritance has come to us on this side of the Jordan to the east." So Moses said to them, "If you will do this, if you will take up arms to go before the Lord for the war, and every armed man of you will pass over the Jordan before the Lord, until he has driven out his enemies from before him and the land is subdued before the Lord; then after that you shall return and be free of obligation to the Lord and to Israel, and this land shall be your possession before the Lord. But if you will not do so, behold, you have sinned against the Lord, and be sure your sin will find you out. Build cities for your little ones and folds for your sheep, and do what you have promised." And the people of Gad and the people of Reuben said to Moses, "Your servants will do as my lord commands. (ESV)

JOSHUA 22: 1 - 6

At that time Joshua summoned the Reubenites and the Gadites and the half-tribe of Manasseh, and said to them, "You have kept all that Moses the servant of the Lord commanded you and have obeyed my voice in all that I have commanded you. You have not forsaken your brothers these many days, down to this day, but have been careful to keep the charge of the Lord your God. And now the Lord your God has given rest to your brothers, as He promised them. Therefore turn and go to your tents in the land where your possession lies, which Moses the servant of the Lord gave you on the other side of the Jordan. Only be very careful to observe the commandment and the law that Moses the servant of the Lord commanded you, to love the Lord your God, and to walk in all His ways and to keep His commandments and to cling to Him and to serve Him with all your heart and with all your soul." So Joshua blessed them and sent them away, and they went to their tents. (ESV)

PRAYER FOCUS:

Help me to show faithfulness to You and to others in all that I do. May I be known as a person of my word, fulfilling what I have promised to do, for Your sake and for the sake of Your great name.

Tammuz Day 20

Reuben and the other tribes who settled on the east side of the Jordan River built an altar on the river bank once they returned home from fulfilling their agreement to help the others take the land. At first, the other tribes didn't understand what the monument meant, and they were offended. Once it was explained, however, it showed a desire on the part of the Reubenites and others to follow God. Sometimes misunderstandings may arise, even among believers, but if our motives are right before God, there is always room for dialogue and ultimately, restoration.

Scripture:

Joshua 22: 10 - 34

And when they came to the region of the Jordan that is in the land of Canaan, the people of Reuben and the people of Gad and the half-tribe of Manasseh built there an altar by the Jordan, an altar of imposing size. And the people of Israel heard it and said, "Behold, the people of Reuben and the people of Gad and the half-tribe of Manasseh have built the altar at the frontier of the land of Canaan, in the region about the Jordan, on the side that belongs to the people of Israel." And when the people of Israel heard of it, the whole assembly of the people of Israel gathered at Shiloh to make war against them.

Then the people of Israel sent to the people of Reuben and the people of Gad and the half-tribe of Manasseh, in the land of Gilead, Phinehas the son of Eleazar the priest, and with him ten chiefs, one from each of the tribal families of Israel, every one of them the head of a family among the clans of Israel. And they came to the people of Reuben, the people of Gad, and the half-tribe of Manasseh, in the land of Gilead, and they said to them, "Thus says the whole congregation of the Lord, 'What is this breach of faith that you have committed against the God of Israel in turning away this day from following the Lord by building yourselves an altar this day in rebellion against the Lord? Have we not had enough of the sin at Peor from which even yet we have not cleansed ourselves, and for which there came a plague upon the congregation of the Lord, that you too must turn away this day from following the Lord? And if you too rebel against the Lord today then tomorrow He will be angry with the whole congregation of Israel. But now, if the land of your possession is unclean, pass over into the Lord's land where the Lord's tabernacle stands, and take for yourselves a possession among us. Only do not rebel against the Lord or make us as rebels by building for yourselves an altar other than the altar of the Lord our God. Did not Achan the son of Zerah break faith in the matter of the devoted things, and wrath fell upon all the congregation of Israel? And he did not perish alone for his iniquity.'"

Then the people of Reuben, the people of Gad, and the half-tribe of Manasseh said in answer to the heads of the families of Israel, "The Mighty One, God, the Lord! The Mighty One, God, the Lord! He knows; and let Israel itself know! If it was in rebellion or in breach of faith against the Lord, do not spare us today for building an altar to turn away from following the Lord. Or if we did so to offer burnt offerings or grain offerings or peace offerings on it, may the Lord Himself take vengeance. No, but we did it from fear that in time to come your children might say to our children, 'What have you to do with the Lord, the God of Israel? For the Lord has made the Jordan a boundary between us and you, you people of Reuben and people of Gad. You have no portion in the Lord.' So your children might make our children cease to worship the Lord. Therefore we said, 'Let us now build an altar, not for burnt offering, nor for sacrifice, but to be a witness between us and you, and between our generations after us, that we do perform the service of the Lord in His presence with our burnt offerings and sacrifices and peace offerings, so your children will not say to our children in time to come, "You have no portion in the Lord."' And we thought, 'If this should be said to us or to our descendants in time to come, we should say, "Behold, the copy of the altar of the Lord, which our fathers made, not for burnt offerings, nor for sacrifice, but to be a witness between us and you."' Far be it from us that we should rebel against the Lord and turn away this day from following the Lord by building an altar for burnt offering, grain offering, or sacrifice, other than the altar of the Lord our God that stands before His tabernacle!"

When Phinehas the priest and the chiefs of the congregation, the heads of the families of Israel who were with him, heard the words that the people of Reuben and the people of Gad and the people of Manasseh spoke, it was good in their eyes. And Phinehas the son of Eleazar the priest said to the people of Reuben and the people of Gad and the people of Manasseh, "Today we know that the Lord is in our midst, because you have not committed this breach of faith against the Lord. Now you have delivered the people of Israel from the hand of the Lord."

Then Phinehas the son of Eleazar the priest, and the chiefs, returned from the people of Reuben and the people of Gad in the land of Gilead to the land of Canaan, to the people of Israel, and brought back word to them. And the report was good in the eyes of the people of Israel. And the people of Israel blessed God and spoke no more of making war against them to destroy the land where the people of Reuben and the people of Gad were settled. The people of Reuben and the people of Gad called the altar Witness, "For," they said, "it is a witness between us that the Lord is God." (ESV)

PRAYER FOCUS:

I pray along with the people of Israel, "The Lord is God!" May my life be a witness for You even as the altar built by the Reubenites was called a 'Witness' for Your great name. When misunderstandings arise, help those involved to have open hearts and ears to hear what the other side meant before jumping to conclusions, and may restoration, in love, always be the ultimate goal.

Tammuz Day 21

There are other Reubenites mentioned in the Bible who showed faithfulness to God. For instance, Reubenites came to Hebron to support David as King of Israel, among them Adina, who is listed as one of David's mighty men.

SCRIPTURE:

1 Chronicles 11: 1 - 3

Then all Israel gathered to David at Hebron and said, "Behold, we are your bone and your flesh. In times past, even when Saul was king, you were the one who led out and brought in Israel; and the Lord your God said to you, 'You shall shepherd My people Israel, and you shall be prince over My people Israel.'" So all the elders of Israel came to the king at Hebron, and David made a covenant with them in Hebron before the Lord; and they anointed David king over Israel, according to the word of the Lord through Samuel.

(NASB)

1 CHRONICLES 11: 10 & 42

Now these are the heads of the mighty men whom David had, who gave him strong support in his kingdom, together with all Israel, to make him king, according to the word of the Lord concerning Israel... Adina the son of Shiza the Reubenite, a chief of the Reubenites, and thirty with him. (NASB)

. . .

PRAYER FOCUS:

I thank You for the example of those who have gone before as faithful witnesses, unafraid to stand up and be counted for You. Help me to learn from them. May I be listed among the 'mighty men' as a person of valour.

Tammuz Day 22

Unfortunately, the tribe of Reuben were also some of the first to turn away from God, and they were subsequently taken captive by the Assyrians. No matter how secure we may feel, we must guard our hearts and our eyes, putting on our breastplate and armour each and every day. It is up to us to choose life, not death, by following God and staying close to Him.

SCRIPTURE:

1 Chronicles 5: 26

So the God of Israel stirred up the spirit of Pul king of Assyria (that is, Tiglath-Pileser king of Assyria), who took the Reubenites, the Gadites and the half-tribe of Manasseh into exile. He took them to Halah, Habor, Hara and the river of Gozan, where they are to this day. (NIV)

DEUTERONOMY 11: 26 - 32

"See, I am setting before you today a blessing and a curse: the blessing, if you listen to the commandments of the Lord your God, which I am commanding you today; and the curse, if you do not listen to the commandments of the Lord your God, but turn aside from the way which I am commanding you today, by following other gods which you have not known. It shall come about, when the Lord your God brings you into the land where you are entering to possess it, that you shall place the blessing on Mount Gerizim and the curse on Mount Ebal. Are they not across the Jordan, west of the way toward the sunset, in the land of the Canaanites who live in the Arabah, opposite Gilgal, beside the oaks of Moreh? For you are about to cross the Jordan to go in to possess the land which the Lord your God is giving you, and you shall possess it and live in it, and you shall be careful to do all the statutes and the judgments which I am setting before you today. (NASB)

Deuteronomy 30: 15 - 19

"See, I have set before you today life and prosperity, and death and adversity; in that I command you today to love the Lord your God, to walk in His ways and to keep His commandments and His statutes and His judgments, that you may live and multiply, and that the Lord your God may bless you in the land where you are entering to possess it. But if your heart turns away and you will not obey, but are drawn away and worship other gods and serve them, I declare to you today that you shall surely perish. You will not prolong your days in the land where you are crossing the Jordan to enter and possess it. I call heaven and earth to witness against you today, that I have set before you life and death, the blessing and the curse. So choose life in order that you may live, you and your descendants, by loving the Lord your God, by obeying His voice, and by holding fast to Him; for this is your life and the length of your days, that you may live in the land which the Lord swore to your fathers, to Abraham, Isaac, and Jacob, to give them."

(NASB)

.   .   .

PRAYER FOCUS:

I choose life today, oh God! Help me to guard my heart by guarding what I take in through my eyes, ears, and other senses. Forgive me for going astray, and enable me to stay on the narrow path that leads to You. Thank You that Your promises are still there for me today. However, I recognize that I must also do my part by remaining faithful to You and to Your Word.

Tammuz Day 23

During the month of Tammuz, the twelve spies were sent out from the camp into the promised land to scope it out and then report back. They returned in the next month, on the ninth of Av, with a bad report, even though there was much to recommend the land. (The ninth of Av was mentioned already on day number 17 as one of significance in Jewish tradition.) When God 'sends us out', it is up to us to see through His eyes, not our own earthly ones.

SCRIPTURE:

Numbers 13: 1- 3 and 17 - 24

The Lord said to Moses, "Send some men to explore the land of Canaan, which I am giving to the Israelites. From each ancestral tribe send one of its leaders." So at the Lord's command Moses sent them out from the Desert of Paran. All of them were leaders of the Israelites...

When Moses sent them to explore Canaan, he said, "Go up through the Negev and on into the hill country. See what the land is like and whether the people who live there are strong or weak, few or many. What kind of land do they live in? Is it good or bad? What kind of towns do they live in? Are they unwalled or fortified? How is the soil? Is it fertile or poor? Are there trees in it or not? Do your best to bring back some of the fruit of the land." (It was the season for the first ripe grapes.)

So they went up and explored the land from the Desert of Zin as far as Rehob, toward Lebo Hamath. They went up through the Negev and came to Hebron, where Ahiman, Sheshai and Talmai, the descendants of Anak, lived. (Hebron had been built seven years before Zoan in Egypt.) When they reached the Valley of Eshkol, they cut off a branch bearing a single cluster of grapes. Two of them carried it on a pole between them, along with some pomegranates and figs. That place was called the Valley of Eshkol because of the cluster of grapes the Israelites cut off there.

(NIV)

NUMBERS 14: 6 - 10a

Joshua son of Nun and Caleb son of Jephunneh, who were among those who had explored the land, tore their clothes and said to the entire Israelite assembly, "The land we passed through and explored is exceedingly good. If the Lord is pleased with us, He will lead us into that land, a land flowing with milk and honey, and will give it to us. Only do not rebel against the Lord. And do not be afraid of the people of the land, because we will devour them. Their protection is gone, but the Lord is with us. Do not be afraid of them." But the whole assembly talked about stoning them.

(NIV)

2 KINGS 6: 17

Then Elisha prayed and said, "Oh Lord, I pray, open his eyes that he may see." And the Lord opened the servant's eyes and he saw; and behold, the mountain was full of horses and chariots of fire all around Elisha. (NASB)

. . .

PRAYER FOCUS:

Help me to trust in You, Lord. Forgive me for the sin of worry and faithlessness. Instead, help me to see with Your eyes and to move forward according to Your direction—without fear!

Tammuz Day 24

Further to yesterday's reading about the spies, we must watch what comes out of our mouths, and confess the best that the Lord has for us. It is up to us to agree with, accept, and embrace God's call, not speak an evil report! It is easy to fall into negativity. However, God wants us to be at peace with who we are and not fall into the trap of speaking evil about ourselves or others. Instead, choose to believe and confess God's promises.

SCRIPTURE:

Ephesians 1: 15 - 23

For this reason, ever since I heard about your faith in the Lord Jesus and your love for all God's people, I have not stopped giving thanks for you, remembering you in my prayers. I keep asking that the God of our Lord Jesus Christ, the glorious Father, may give you the Spirit of wisdom and revelation, so that you may know Him better. I pray that the eyes of your heart may be enlightened in order that you may know the hope to which He has called you, the riches of His glorious inheritance in His holy people, and His incomparably great power for us who believe. That power is the same as the mighty strength He exerted when He raised Christ from the dead and seated Him at His right hand in the heavenly realms, far above all rule and authority, power and dominion, and every name that is invoked, not only in the present age but also in the one to come. And God placed all things under His feet and appointed Him to be head over everything for the church, which is His body, the fullness of Him who fills everything in every way. (NIV)

PRAYER FOCUS:

I agree with and speak positive words over the destiny that You have for me! Forgive me for negative self-talk, or for negatively speaking about others. Instead, show me how to pray the scriptures over those I love and over various situations. Thank You for Your great and precious promises, and help me to memorize Your Word so that I can access it in times of need.

Tammuz Day 25

Covenant rights are linked with power and strength, an important aspect of the tribe of Reuben and the month of Tammuz. It is important to take note of all of our alignments. Although we seldom use the word 'covenant' anymore, we must notice all of our 'handshakes'—both real and symbolic, and be careful not to align ourselves without first consulting the Lord.

SCRIPTURE:

Hebrews 8: 7 - 12

For if there had been nothing wrong with that first covenant, no place would have been sought for another. But God found fault with the people and said, "The days are coming, declares the Lord, when I will make a new covenant with the people of Israel and with the people of Judah. It will not be like the covenant I made with their ancestors when I took them by the hand to lead them out of Egypt, because they did not remain faithful to my covenant, and I turned away from them," declares the Lord. "This is the covenant I will establish with the people of Israel after that time," declares the Lord. "I will put my laws in their minds and write them on their hearts. I will be their God, and they will be my people. No longer will they teach their neighbour, or say to one another, 'Know the Lord,' because they will all know me, from the least of them to the greatest. For I will forgive their wickedness and will remember their sins no more." (NIV)

. . .

SONG OF SOLOMON 5: 2 - 9

I slept but my heart was awake.
Listen! My beloved is knocking:
"Open to me, my sister, my darling,
my dove, my flawless one.
My head is drenched with dew,
my hair with the dampness of the night."
I have taken off my robe -
must I put it on again?
I have washed my feet -
must I soil them again?
My beloved thrust his hand through the latch-opening;
my heart began to pound for him.
I arose to open for my beloved,
and my hands dripped with myrrh,
my fingers with flowing myrrh,
on the handles of the bolt.
I opened for my beloved,
but my beloved had left; he was gone.
My heart sank at his departure.
I looked for him but did not find him.
I called him but he did not answer.
The watchmen found me
as they made their rounds in the city.
They beat me, they bruised me;
they took away my cloak,
those watchmen of the walls!
Daughters of Jerusalem, I charge you -
if you find my beloved,
what will you tell him?
Tell him I am faint with love.

Friends
How is your beloved better than others,
most beautiful of women?
How is your beloved better than others,
that you so charge us? (NIV)

PRAYER FOCUS:
Make me aware of the spiritual significance of every covenant and contract I come into. I place every contract, business deal, friendship, relationship, and any other alignment in Your hands, oh God, and ask for Your guidance.

Tammuz Day 26

As a reminder of God's great commission and the vision of His holiness, here is another account of a heavenly vision, this time by the prophet Isaiah. Notice the similarities to those of Ezekiel and John. The Lord seems to be sending the same message, and throughout we are to worship Him in all His glory and majesty.

SCRIPTURE:

Isaiah 6: 1 - 8

In the year that King Uzziah died, I saw the Lord, high and exalted, seated on a throne; and the train of His robe filled the temple. Above Him were seraphim, each with six wings: With two wings they covered their faces, with two they covered their feet, and with two they were flying. And they were calling to one another, "Holy, holy, holy is the Lord Almighty; the whole earth is full of his glory."

At the sound of their voices the doorposts and thresholds shook and the temple was filled with smoke.

"Woe to me!" I cried. "I am ruined! For I am a man of unclean lips, and I live among a people of unclean lips, and my eyes have seen the King, the Lord Almighty."

Then one of the seraphim flew to me with a live coal in his hand, which he had taken with tongs from the altar. With it he touched my mouth and said, "See, this has touched your lips; your guilt is taken away and your sin atoned for."

Then I heard the voice of the Lord saying, "Whom shall I send? And who will go for Us?"

And I said, "Here am I. Send me!" (NIV)

.   .   .

Thank You again for Your glory and power. With the prophet I cry out, "Here I am, send me!" Make me willing to go where You send me and to speak the words You give me to speak. May I continue to look to You for strength, for You are all powerful and worthy of all praise.

Tammuz Day 27

As we continue moving forward this year, it is important to watch our progress and make adjustments as needed. We can learn from the mistakes of the past and make different choices as we advance.

SCRIPTURE:

John 8: 2 - 11

Early in the morning He came again to the temple. All the people came to Him, and He sat down and taught them. The scribes and the Pharisees brought a woman who had been caught in adultery, and placing her in the midst they said to Him, "Teacher, this woman has been caught in the act of adultery. Now in the Law, Moses commanded us to stone such women. So what do you say?" This they said to test Him, that they might have some charge to bring against Him. Jesus bent down and wrote with His finger on the ground. And as they continued to ask Him, He stood up and said to them, "Let him who is without sin among you be the first to throw a stone at her." And once more He bent down and wrote on the ground. But when they heard it, they went away one by one, beginning with the older ones, and Jesus was left alone with the woman standing before Him. Jesus stood up and said to her, "Woman, where are they? Has no one condemned you?" She said, "No one, Lord." And Jesus said, "Neither do I condemn you; go, and from now on sin no more." (ESV)

.   .   .

Luke 7: 41 - 47

"A certain moneylender had two debtors. One owed five hundred denarii, and the other fifty. When they could not pay, he cancelled the debt of both. Now which of them will love him more?" Simon answered, "The one, I suppose, for whom he cancelled the larger debt." And He (Jesus) said to him, "You have judged rightly." Then turning toward the woman He said to Simon, "Do you see this woman? I entered your house; you gave me no water for my feet, but she has wet my feet with her tears and wiped them with her hair. You gave me no kiss, but from the time I came in she has not ceased to kiss my feet. You did not anoint my head with oil, but she has anointed my feet with ointment. Therefore I tell you, her sins, which are many, are forgiven - for she loved much. But he who is forgiven little, loves little." (ESV)

Prayer focus:

Thank You that Your favour lasts a lifetime. We are not stuck in our sins, but can move forward with You each day as a brand new person. Help me to learn from the mistakes of the past—both my own and those of others—so that I may continue to grow in righteousness.

Tammuz Day 28

Sometimes we build walls around ourselves. Usually these walls are for protection from what we think may hurt us. Self-doubt, pity, fear and pride come to mind. Like the women in yesterday's stories, we must learn to be vulnerable before God.

SCRIPTURE:

Psalm 118

Give thanks to the Lord, for He is good;

His love endures forever.

Let Israel say:

"His love endures forever."

Let the house of Aaron say:

"His love endures forever."

Let those who fear the Lord say:

"His love endures forever."

When hard pressed, I cried to the Lord;

He brought me into a spacious place.

The Lord is with me; I will not be afraid.

What can mere mortals do to me?

The Lord is with me; He is my helper.

I look in triumph on my enemies.

It is better to take refuge in the Lord

than to trust in humans.

It is better to take refuge in the Lord

than to trust in princes.

All the nations surrounded me,

but in the name of the Lord I cut them down.

They surrounded me on every side,

but in the name of the Lord I cut them down.
They swarmed around me like bees,
but they were consumed as quickly as burning thorns;
in the name of the Lord I cut them down.
I was pushed back and about to fall,
but the Lord helped me.
The Lord is my strength and my defense;
He has become my salvation.
Shouts of joy and victory
resound in the tents of the righteous:
"The Lord's right hand has done mighty things!
The Lord's right hand is lifted high;
the Lord's right hand has done mighty things!"
I will not die but live,
and will proclaim what the Lord has done.
The Lord has chastened me severely,
but He has not given me over to death.
Open for me the gates of the righteous;
I will enter and give thanks to the Lord.
This is the gate of the Lord
through which the righteous may enter.
I will give You thanks, for You answered me;
You have become my salvation.
The stone the builders rejected
has become the cornerstone;
the Lord has done this,
and it is marvellous in our eyes.
The Lord has done it this very day;
let us rejoice today and be glad.
Lord, save us!
Lord, grant us success!

Blessed is he who comes in the name of the Lord.
From the house of the Lord we bless you.
The Lord is God,
and He has made His light shine on us.
With boughs in hand, join in the festal procession
up to the horns of the altar.
You are my God, and I will praise You;
You are my God, and I will exalt You.
Give thanks to the Lord, for He is good;
His love endures forever. (NIV)

PRAYER FOCUS:

I declare today that every wall of fear, pride, shame or anything else that I have allowed to surround me, will be broken down in the name of Jesus. Lord, I want to be vulnerable when it comes to You, but may Your Holy Spirit surround and protect me as I learn to walk closer to You. You are good, and Your love endures forever!

Tammuz Day 29

With the Psalmist, may we continue to worship the Lord first, no matter our circumstances.

SCRIPTURE:

Psalm 46

God is our refuge and strength,
an ever-present help in trouble.
Therefore we will not fear, though the earth give way
and the mountains fall into the heart of the sea,
though its waters roar and foam
and the mountains quake with their surging.
There is a river whose streams make glad
the city of God,
the holy place where the Most High dwells.
God is within her, she will not fall;
God will help her at break of day.
Nations are in uproar, kingdoms fall;
He lifts His voice, the earth melts.
The Lord Almighty is with us;
the God of Jacob is our fortress.
Come and see what the Lord has done,
the desolations He has brought on the earth.
He makes wars cease
to the ends of the earth.
He breaks the bow and shatters the spear;
He burns the shields with fire.
He says, "Be still, and know that I am God;
I will be exalted among the nations,
I will be exalted in the earth."

The Lord Almighty is with us;
the God of Jacob is our fortress. (NIV)

PRAYER FOCUS:

Thank You, Lord, that You are my fortress, and that all things are subject to You. I worship You today in spirit and truth, and entrust my life and the lives of my loved ones into Your care as we move into the next month.

A V - Month 5
The Month of Simeon
30 days - July/August

As noted last month, the history of the children of Israel is not at its peak during the summer months. In fact, the month of Av is considered the 'low point' in the Hebrew calendar. However, God's redemption is always available when we choose to have faith in Him. As you will see, the message of Av is clear: repent of the sins of the past so that the doors of destruction cannot open again. Choose to break all iniquitous patterns and habits; choose to believe God's promises; choose to enter into God's blessing. Simply put, choose faith over unbelief.

Av Day 1 - Rosh Chodesh

This month is about making right choices. God never treats us like puppets on a string, but allows us the choice to follow His plan. This applies to every aspect of our lives as believers, including making the choice to honour Him with our firstfruits. The children of Israel knew these principles well and followed them when they entered the promised land. Jericho was the first of the cities that they defeated once crossing the Jordan river, and as such, all of the plunder was to be dedicated to the Lord. They were not to take the spoils for themselves, even though in future conquests they were allowed to do so. When Achan disobeyed this principle, there were disastrous results for all the people. God's punishment might seem harsh and extreme to us today, but remember that He is righteous and holy. His ways are always just—a sobering thought.

Scripture:

Joshua 6: 15 - 21

On the seventh day, they got up at daybreak and marched around the city seven times in the same manner, except that on that day they circled the city seven times. The seventh time around, when the priests sounded the trumpet blast, Joshua commanded the army, "Shout! For the Lord has given you the city! The city and all that is in it are to be devoted to the Lord. Only Rahab the prostitute and all who are with her in her house shall be spared, because she hid the spies we sent. But keep away from the devoted things, so that you will not bring about your own destruction by taking any of them. Otherwise you will make the camp of Israel liable to destruction and bring trouble on it. All the silver and gold and the articles of bronze and iron are sacred to the Lord and must go into his treasury."

When the trumpets sounded, the army shouted, and at the sound of the trumpet, when the men gave a loud shout, the wall collapsed; so everyone charged straight in, and they took the city. They devoted the city to the Lord and destroyed with the sword every living thing in it - men and women, young and old, cattle, sheep and donkeys. (NIV)

Joshua 7: 10 - 25

The Lord said to Joshua, "Stand up! What are you doing down on your face? Israel has sinned; they have violated My covenant, which I commanded them to keep. They have taken some of the devoted things; they have stolen, they have lied, they have put them with their own possessions. That is why the Israelites cannot stand against their enemies; they turn their backs and run because they have been made liable to destruction. I will not be with you anymore unless you destroy whatever among you is devoted to destruction.

"Go, consecrate the people. Tell them, 'Consecrate yourselves in preparation for tomorrow; for this is what the Lord, the God of Israel, says: There are devoted things among you, Israel. You cannot stand against your enemies until you remove them.

" 'In the morning, present yourselves tribe by tribe. The tribe the Lord chooses shall come forward clan by clan; the clan the Lord chooses shall come forward family by family; and the family the Lord chooses shall come forward man by man. Whoever is caught with the devoted things shall be destroyed by fire, along with all that belongs to him. He has violated the covenant of the Lord and has done an outrageous thing in Israel!' "

Early the next morning Joshua had Israel come forward by tribes, and Judah was chosen. The clans of Judah came forward, and the Zerahites were chosen. He had the clan of the Zerahites come forward by families, and Zimri was chosen. Joshua had his family come forward man by man, and Achan son of Karmi, the son of Zimri, the son of Zerah, of the tribe of Judah, was chosen.

Then Joshua said to Achan, "My son, give glory to the Lord, the God of Israel, and honour Him. Tell me what you have done; do not hide it from me."

Achan replied, "It is true! I have sinned against the Lord, the God of Israel. This is what I have done: When I saw in the plunder a beautiful robe from Babylonia, two hundred shekels of silver and a bar of gold weighing fifty shekels, I coveted them and took them. They are hidden in the ground inside my tent, with the silver underneath."

So Joshua sent messengers, and they ran to the tent, and there it was, hidden in his tent, with the silver underneath. They took the things from the tent, brought them to Joshua and all the Israelites and spread them out before the Lord.

Then Joshua, together with all Israel, took Achan son of Zerah, the silver, the robe, the gold bar, his sons and daughters, his cattle, donkeys and sheep, his tent and all that he had, to the Valley of Achor. Joshua said, "Why have you brought this trouble on us? The Lord will bring trouble on you today."

Then all Israel stoned him, and after they had stoned the rest, they burned them. Over Achan they heaped up a large pile of rocks, which remains to this day. Then the Lord turned from his fierce anger. Therefore that place has been called the Valley of Achor ever since. (NIV)

PRAYER FOCUS:

Lord, restore in me, and in all Your people, a holy fear of You, for You are the righteous judge and will not be mocked. Thank You that You provided a way of atonement through Jesus' blood so that we would not have to suffer the kind of punishment that Achan did. Help me to be mindful of keeping Your ways and listening to Your instructions, however, for I know that Your principles have not changed, even as You have not changed. With this in mind, show me how I can honour You with my firstfruits in a modern context.

Av Day 2

As already discussed, each month of the Hebrew calendar corresponds with a letter of the alphabet, which in turn is found in Psalm 119, David's acrostic celebrating God's Word. The month of Av is represented by the letter TET or TETH. The symbol itself looks like a spiral or vortex, and the meaning is to knot together, twist, spin or interweave. It may also be representational of a womb, which fits in that we are 'knit together' in our mothers' wombs. God's Word must be interwoven into the very fabric of our lives, and is what 'knots' us together with Christ.

Scripture:

Psalm 119: 65 - 72
Do good to Your servant according to Your word, Lord.
Teach me knowledge and good judgment,
for I trust Your commands.
Before I was afflicted I went astray,
but now I obey Your word.
You are good, and what You do is good;
teach me Your decrees.
Though the arrogant have smeared me with lies,
I keep Your precepts with all my heart.
Their hearts are callous and unfeeling,
but I delight in Your law.
It was good for me to be afflicted
so that I might learn Your decrees.
The law from Your mouth is more precious to me
than thousands of pieces of silver and gold. (NIV)

. . .

PRAYER FOCUS:

Lord, help me to tie myself to You so tightly that I cannot be removed. Open Your Word to me like never before as I study and meditate on it, weaving it into the very fabric of my life. Thank You for any difficult circumstances and trials that I may have had to go through, or that I am going through right now, for these are what draw me close to You and help me to grow. Help me to see them as opportunities for You to shine Your glory through my life. May I always be a person of integrity, no matter what others may say about me.

Av Day 3

As we saw yesterday, the idea of being knit together with the Lord is one that is prominent this month. David celebrated the fact that he was knit together in his mother's womb. God knows us inside and out—something to rest in and meditate on, for we are fearfully and wonderfully made. Nothing in our lives takes God by surprise.

Scripture:

Psalm 139
O Lord, You have searched me and known me!
You know when I sit down and when I rise up;
You discern my thoughts from afar.
You search out my path and my lying down
and are acquainted with all my ways.
Even before a word is on my tongue,
behold, O Lord, You know it altogether.
You hem me in, behind and before,
and lay Your hand upon me.
Such knowledge is too wonderful for me;
it is high; I cannot attain it.
Where shall I go from Your Spirit?
Or where shall I flee from Your presence?
If I ascend to heaven, You are there!
If I make my bed in Sheol, You are there!
If I take the wings of the morning
and dwell in the uttermost parts of the sea,
even there Your hand shall lead me,
and Your right hand shall hold me.
If I say, "Surely the darkness shall cover me,

and the light about me be night,"
even the darkness is not dark to You;
the night is bright as the day,
for darkness is as light with You.
For You formed my inward parts;
You knitted me together in my mother's womb.
I praise You, for I am fearfully and wonderfully made.
Wonderful are Your works;
my soul knows it very well.
My frame was not hidden from You,
when I was being made in secret,
intricately woven in the depths of the earth.
Your eyes saw my unformed substance;
in Your book were written, every one of them,
the days that were formed for me,
when as yet there was none of them.
How precious to me are Your thoughts, O God!
How vast is the sum of them!
If I would count them, they are more than the sand.
I awake, and I am still with You.
Oh that You would slay the wicked, O God!
O men of blood, depart from me!
They speak against You with malicious intent;
Your enemies take Your name in vain.
Do I not hate those who hate You, O Lord?
And do I not loathe those who rise up against You?
I hate them with complete hatred;
I count them my enemies.
Search me, O God, and know my heart!
Try me and know my thoughts!
And see if there be any grievous way in me,

and lead me in the way everlasting! (ESV)

Prayer focus:
Thank You, Lord, that You formed me and know me through and through. I am fearfully and wonderfully made, and I praise You today for Your omnipotence and omniscience. Nothing can be hidden from You, Lord, and so I dedicate all that I am to You. Root out anything that is not pleasing to You: generational curses, any unclean thing that has attached itself to me spiritually, or any other bondage that I have allowed into my life through any means, be it intentional or unintentional. Guide my steps through the rest of this month and this year, in Jesus mighty name.

Av Day 4

In keeping with the idea of being knit together in the womb, a sense of metamorphosis is emphasized this month. Change is inevitable. A pregnant woman can keep her pregnancy secret for a while, but it will eventually be known. Before that happens, though, she will experience many signs that may be known only by her—many changes are taking place even before she is 'showing'. So it is in the spiritual realm. Things are happening—beginning—and even if we cannot see them clearly now, they will take place at God's appointed time.

SCRIPTURE:
Isaiah 44: 1 - 5
But now listen, Jacob, my servant,
Israel, whom I have chosen.
This is what the Lord says -
He who made you, who formed you in the womb,
and who will help you:
Do not be afraid, Jacob, my servant,
Jeshurun whom I have chosen.
For I will pour water on the thirsty land,
and streams on the dry ground;
I will pour out my Spirit on your offspring,
and my blessing on your descendants.
They will spring up like grass in a meadow,
like poplar trees by flowing streams.
Some will say, 'I belong to the Lord';
others will call themselves by the name of Jacob;
still others will write on their hand, 'The Lord's,'

and will take the name Israel. (NIV)

Prayer focus:

Thank You that each of Your promises will take place at the appointed time. I bring my family members forward today and claim the promise that they will 'spring up like grass in the meadow'. Pour out Your thirst quenching Spirit upon the dry ground of my life—my family, my job, my finances—any area that needs a touch from You. Thank You that You are moving; that I can trust You to fulfill Your Word in due season as I wait upon You and trust in Your timing.

Av Day 5

The contractions and pain of childbirth are another aspect of this 'birthing' season that must be mentioned. As contractions take place in the heavenly realms so they are mirrored in the earth and in our own lives. We may go through pains as in labour, but we must keep in mind that this is a natural course of action and keep our focus on God's steadfastness and faithfulness. There will be great reward at the end of our pain and suffering if we only wait upon Him and allow Him to see us through.

SCRIPTURE:

Isaiah 42: 1 - 16
Behold My servant, whom I uphold,
My chosen, in whom My soul delights;
I have put My Spirit upon Him;
He will bring forth justice to the nations.
He will not cry aloud or lift up His voice,
or make it heard in the street;
A bruised reed He will not break,
and a faintly burning wick He will not quench;
He will faithfully bring forth justice.
He will not grow faint or be discouraged
till He has established justice in the earth;
and the coastlands wait for His law.
Thus says God, the Lord,
who created the heavens and stretched them out,
who spread out the earth and what comes from it,
who gives breath to the people on it
and spirit to those who walk in it:

"I am the Lord; I have called you in righteousness;
I will take you by the hand and keep you;
I will give you as a covenant for the people,
a light for the nations,
to open the eyes that are blind,
to bring out the prisoners from the dungeon,
from the prison those who sit in darkness.
I am the Lord; that is My name;
My glory I give to no other,
nor My praise to carved idols.
Behold, the former things have come to pass,
and new things I now declare;
before they spring forth
I tell you of them."
Sing to the Lord a new song,
His praise from the end of the earth,
you who go down to the sea, and all that fills it,
the coastlands and their inhabitants.
Let the desert and its cities lift up their voice,
the villages that Kedar inhabits;
let the habitants of Sela sing for joy,
let them shout from the top of the mountains.
Let them give glory to the Lord,
and declare His praise in the coastlands.
The Lord goes out like a mighty man,
like a man of war He stirs up His zeal;
He cries out, He shouts aloud,
He shows Himself mighty against His foes.
For a long time I have held My peace;
I have kept still and restrained Myself;
now I will cry out like a woman in labor;

I will gasp and pant.
I will lay waste mountains and hills,
and dry up all their vegetation;
I will turn the rivers into islands,
and dry up the pools.
And I will lead the blind
in a way that they do not know,
in paths that they have not known
I will guide them.
I will turn the darkness before them into light,
the rough places into level ground.
These are the things I do,
and I do not forsake them. (ESV)

PRAYER FOCUS:

Thank You that long before Jesus came to earth in human form You spoke about Him in scripture so that we could see and rejoice at the fulfillment of prophecy. Enlighten me, both mind and spirit, as I read Your Word, so that I can see You throughout scripture and be built up in faith. Help me to cling to You, even in difficult circumstances, for in due season You will bring about joy at the fulfillment of Your righteous plans. Begin a new thing in my life and in Your church—a spiritual birthing and renewal. Whatever the pain and discomfort, I pray that You would see me through this time so that I may rejoice in the newness that is coming, having faith to remain steadfast through every trial or circumstance.

Av Day 6

Just as a woman's pregnancy will someday be revealed, so all God's plans will be revealed to mankind. This has happened over and over again through the prophetic word found in the Bible. In the book of Amos, the prophetic word is likened to a lion roaring. Did you know that in the movie business, sound engineers often add the sound of a lion's roar to the background of a storm to give it more substance and intensity? Once the sound of the lion's roar has been released, it is up to those who hear it to decide whether to act on it or not; whether to walk in faith or unbelief.

SCRIPTURE:

Amos 3: 7 - 8
For the Lord God does nothing
without revealing His secret
to His servants the prophets.
The lion has roared;
who will not fear?
The Lord God has spoken;
who can but prophesy? (ESV)

ISAIAH 24: 14 - 16
They raise their voices, they shout for joy;
from the west they acclaim the Lord's majesty.
Therefore in the east give glory to the Lord;
exalt the name of the Lord, the God of Israel,
in the islands of the sea.

From the ends of the earth we hear singing:
"Glory to the Righteous One." (NIV)

PRAYER FOCUS:

I praise You today, oh God, for You are worthy of all praise! Along with those who sing Your praise I cry out, "Glory to the Righteous One!" Speak through Your prophets. Like a lion roaring, may the sound of Your Word echo in my heart and out to those around me. Open my ears to hear and understand Your Word; make known to me Your secrets and may I be obedient to You. I choose to act in faith today, not unbelief, and march forward to Your call upon my spirit, in Jesus name.

Av Day 7

Sometimes things must be destroyed in order for them to be built up again. We've probably all experienced a time when it was better to just start a project over rather than try to salvage it. The idea of destruction for reconstruction is a recurring one this month. Thankfully, we are already brand new creatures in Christ!

Scripture:

John 2: 18 - 22

The Jews then responded to Him, "What sign can you show us to prove your authority to do all this?"

Jesus answered them, "Destroy this temple, and I will raise it again in three days."

They replied, "It has taken forty-six years to build this temple, and you are going to raise it in three days?" But the temple He had spoken of was His body. After He was raised from the dead, His disciples recalled what He had said. Then they believed the scripture and the words that Jesus had spoken. (NIV)

Isaiah 48: 6 - 7

You have heard; look at all this.
And you, will you not declare it?
I proclaim to you new things from this time,
Even hidden things which you have not known.
They are created now and not long ago;
And before today you have not heard them,

So that you will not say, 'Behold, I knew them.' (NASB)

2 Corinthians 5: 17

Therefore, if anyone is in Christ, he is a new creation. The old has passed away; behold, the new has come. (ESV)

Isaiah 5: 20 - 24

Woe to those who call evil good and good evil,
who put darkness for light and light for darkness,
who put bitter for sweet and sweet for bitter.
Woe to those who are wise in their own eyes
and clever in their own sight.
Woe to those who are heroes at drinking wine
and champions at mixing drinks,
who acquit the guilty for a bribe,
but deny justice to the innocent.
Therefore, as tongues of fire lick up straw
and as dry grass sinks down in the flames,
so their roots will decay
and their flowers blow away like dust;
for they have rejected the law of the Lord Almighty
and spurned the word of the Holy One of Israel. (NIV)

Prayer focus:

Thank You for the brand new covenant of Jesus' blood, and that He was raised again on the third day for the remission of sins. Thank You that when we accept You,

You demolish our old lives and make us brand new creatures in Christ. Help me to put aside every old habit and all old ways that are not pleasing to You, and instead, be a brand new creation, rebuilt from the ground up for You, choosing life over death, good over evil, and faith over unbelief.

Av Day 8

The literal meaning of the word 'Av' is 'father' whose root also means 'to will' or 'to desire'. This month is a time for the divine will of the Father to be carried out. It was His plan during this month to bless His children, but because of unbelief when they rejected the report brought back by the spies, the blessing was postponed as the children of Israel were disciplined for a time.

SCRIPTURE:

1 Thessalonians 2: 11 - 12

For you know how, like a father with his children, we exhorted each one of you and encouraged you and charged you to walk in a manner worthy of God, who calls you into His own kingdom and glory. (ESV)

PROVERBS 3: 11 - 12

My son, do not reject the discipline of the Lord or loathe His reproof, for whom the Lord loves He reproves, even as a father corrects the son in whom he delights. (NASB)

HEBREWS 12:11

No discipline seems pleasant at the time, but painful. Later on, however, it produces a harvest of righteousness and peace for those who have been trained by it. (NIV)

. . .

PRAYER FOCUS:

Like an earthly father, You love us enough to discipline us when needed. Help me to accept Your reproof and to learn from it. Show me where I need to make changes, where I need to repent, and where I need to just trust and wait on You. Thank You that You are a God of second chances and that Your discipline does not last a lifetime, but is meant for my good.

Av Day 9

According to Jewish tradition, the ninth day of Av is a day of disaster and destruction, and in most Jewish households it is a day of fasting and prayer. It is the lowest point in the Hebrew calendar—a time of mourning because of calamity. It all started when the spies returned from their journey, and ten of them gave a bad report instead of trusting God for the victory. As we know, this had disastrous results, and the children of Israel ended up wandering in the desert for another forty years until that entire generation—all except Caleb and Joshua, the two righteous spies—died. Of course, we do not believe in superstition, but we are aware that sin has consequences.

SCRIPTURE:

Numbers 13: 25 - 33

At the end of forty days they returned from exploring the land. They came back to Moses and Aaron and the whole Israelite community at Kadesh in the Desert of Paran. There they reported to them and to the whole assembly and showed them the fruit of the land. They gave Moses this account: "We went into the land to which you sent us, and it does flow with milk and honey! Here is its fruit. But the people who live there are powerful, and the cities are fortified and very large. We even saw descendants of Anak there. The Amalekites live in the Negev; the Hittites, Jebusites and Amorites live in the hill country; and the Canaanites live near the sea and along the Jordan."

Then Caleb silenced the people before Moses and

said, "We should go up and take possession of the land, for we can certainly do it."

But the men who had gone up with him said, "We can't attack those people; they are stronger than we are." And they spread among the Israelites a bad report about the land they had explored. They said, "The land we explored devours those living in it. All the people we saw there are of great size. We saw the Nephilim there (the descendants of Anak come from the Nephilim). We seemed like grasshoppers in our own eyes, and we looked the same to them." (NIV)

NUMBERS 14: 26 - 35

And the Lord spoke to Moses and to Aaron, saying, "How long shall this wicked congregation grumble against me? I have heard the grumblings of the people of Israel, which they grumble against Me. Say to them, 'As I live, declares the Lord, what you have said in My hearing I will do to you: your dead bodies shall fall in this wilderness, and of all your number, listed in the census from twenty years old and upward, who have grumbled against Me, not one shall come into the land where I swore that I would make you dwell, except Caleb the son of Jephunneh and Joshua the son of Nun. But your little ones, who you said would become a prey, I will bring in, and they shall know the land that you have rejected. But as for you, your dead bodies shall fall in this wilderness. And your children shall be shepherds in the wilderness forty years and shall suffer for your faithlessness, until the last of your dead bodies lies in the wilderness. According to the number of the days in which you spied out the land, forty days, a year for each day, you shall bear your iniquity forty years, and you shall know My displeasure.' I, the Lord, have spoken. Surely this will I do to all this wicked congregation who are gathered together against Me: in this wilderness they shall come to a full end, and there they shall die." (ESV)

PRAYER FOCUS:

Forgive me for the times I have been disobedient or when I have allowed disbelief to cloud my judgement instead of trusting in You. I repent before You today, and come before Your mercy seat in an attitude of humility. Help me to trust You and to choose faith over unbelief. Break any curse that my own unbelief may have set in motion, in Jesus name.

Av Day 10

As we saw yesterday, the month of Av was originally supposed to be the month that the children of Israel entered the Promised Land. Instead, they chose unbelief over trusting in God. They gave a negative confession instead of relying on God's strength. As the book of Hebrews explains, they refused to take God at His promises, lacking faith. The result was mourning and destruction. Because of their disobedience, they spent forty years in the wilderness, wandering from place to place.

SCRIPTURE:

Hebrews 3: 7 - 19 and 4: 1 - 2

Therefore, as the Holy Spirit says, "Today, if you hear His voice, do not harden your hearts as in the rebellion, on the day of testing in the wilderness, where your fathers put Me to the test and saw My works for forty years. Therefore I was provoked with that generation, and said, 'They always go astray in their heart; they have not known My ways.' As I swore in My wrath, 'They shall not enter My rest.'"

Take care, brothers, lest there be in any of you an evil, unbelieving heart, leading you to fall away from the living God. But exhort one another every day, as long as it is called "today," that none of you may be hardened by the deceitfulness of sin. For we have come to share in Christ, if indeed we hold our original confidence firm to the end. As it is said, "Today, if you hear His voice, do not harden your hearts as in the rebellion."

For who were those who heard and yet rebelled? Was it not all those who left Egypt led by Moses? And with whom was He provoked for forty years? Was it not with those who sinned, whose bodies fell in the wilderness? And to whom did He swear that they would not enter His rest, but to those who were disobedient?

Therefore, while the promise of entering His rest still stands, let us fear lest any of you should seem to have failed to reach it. For good news came to us just as to them, but the message they heard did not benefit them, because they were not united by faith with those who listened. So we see that they were unable to enter because of unbelief. (ESV)

PRAYER FOCUS:

Soften my heart toward You and to Your voice of instruction, that I might not fall away into unbelief. Help me to encourage and exhort others, as You lead, so that they will also stay the course. I willingly submit to Your righteous discipline and ask for Your mercy so that I can keep my heart pure before You. Forgive me for any stubbornness that wants to linger as I surrender everything, including my pride, over to You.

Av Day 11

Unfortunately, the nation of Israel repeated the same pattern of negativity and unbelief over and over again. When Jesus came, they saw and even tasted the good fruit of His coming, yet chose unbelief over faith. God continues to give us choices, too. We can choose to receive the curse through unbelief and negative confession, or we can break the curse and choose the blessing. We must believe God's promises and then enter into His blessing by having faith.

Scripture:

John 12: 37 - 42

Even after Jesus had performed so many signs in their presence, they still would not believe in Him. This was to fulfill the word of Isaiah the prophet:

"Lord, who has believed our message and to whom has the arm of the Lord been revealed?"

For this reason they could not believe, because, as Isaiah says elsewhere:

"He has blinded their eyes and hardened their hearts, so they can neither see with their eyes, nor understand with their hearts, nor turn - and I would heal them."

Isaiah said this because he saw Jesus' glory and spoke about Him. Yet at the same time many even among the leaders believed in Him. But because of the Pharisees they would not openly acknowledge their faith for fear they would be put out of the synagogue; for they loved human praise more than praise from God. (NIV)

.   .   .

PRAYER FOCUS:

Forgive me for negative confessions over myself, the church, or other people that may have set in motion a pattern of unbelief. Reveal and break all negative patterns in my life, especially patterns of speech: sarcasm, a sharp tongue, unseemly language, criticism, gossip, argumentativeness, defensiveness, unbelief and others. Continue to reveal Yourself to me through Your Holy Spirit, and may my eyes ever be open to You and my heart soft toward You and Your Word. I break any curses that may be over me or over my family. Reveal them specifically to me so that I may pray more effectively. I confess Your goodness and redemption over me and my household from this day forward. I choose life this day! I choose faith in You. I choose the blessing and not the curse, in Jesus name.

Av Day 12

Unbelief can become a pattern, leading to a 'merry-go-round' of negative consequences. As we've seen, this was the case with the children of Israel. However, iniquitous patterns can be broken. Even generational curses have no hold over us when we call on Jesus and allow His cleansing power to change those patterns once and for all. We do not need to live in an ever swirling eddy of fear, doubt, and anxiety, destined to suffer again and again because of our sin. Let Jesus break the cycle!

SCRIPTURE:

2 Corinthians 10: 4 - 5

The weapons we fight with are not the weapons of the world. On the contrary, they have divine power to demolish strongholds. We demolish arguments and every pretension that sets itself up against the knowledge of God, and we take captive every thought to make it obedient to Christ. (NIV)

GALATIANS 5: 1

It was for freedom that Christ set us free; therefore keep standing firm and do not be subject again to a yoke of slavery. (NASB)

PRAYER FOCUS:

Lord, identify those iniquitous patterns that have kept me enslaved—whether they be patterns of negativity, doubt, unnecessary worry or even generational sins that have held me and my family captive to their vices. I claim victory over every generational curse in the name of Jesus and declare that I will move forward from this day onward in new patterns of praise, righteousness and full reliance on You. I take captive every thought in Jesus name, and choose this day to live as a victorious child of the light.

Av Day 13

Av is the month of Simeon, who was the second son of Jacob. His name means 'to hear'. When Leah saw that she had borne Jacob a second son, she felt that the Lord had heard her prayer. Av is a month to hear and understand. Again, it is a choice. If God gives a word, we must choose whether to listen or not. We must also choose whether what has been given is from God or is from another source, such as our own desires, Satan, or those who would want to harm us.

SCRIPTURE:

Genesis 29: 33

She (Leah) conceived again, and when she gave birth to a son she said, "Because the Lord heard that I am not loved, He gave me this one too." So she named him Simeon. (NIV)

JOHN 10: 3- 5

The gatekeeper opens the gate for him, and the sheep listen to his voice. He calls his own sheep by name and leads them out. When he has brought out all his own, he goes on ahead of them, and his sheep follow him because they know his voice. But they will never follow a stranger; in fact, they will run away from him because they do not recognize a stranger's voice."

(NIV)

.   .   .

<u>P<small>RAYER</small> <small>FOCUS</small></u>:

Lord, I pray that I would be in tune with You so that I would recognize Your voice above all others and not heed the voice of another. Help me to hear You, to pay attention, and to obey. Continue to reveal to me any patterns that need to be broken in my life, in Jesus name.

Av Day 14

It is up to us to listen to what the Holy Spirit is saying. Most often it is through His Word, but sometimes it is through prophetic utterances, or the still small voice that He uses to speak to each one of us individually. Being in tune with God and recognizing His voice is key, as is acting on what He says. Like the children of Israel, we have the choice to listen and obey, to ignore it, or to act in unbelief. God always gives us a choice. He will never force His will on us.

Scripture:

Psalm 106: 24 - 27
Then they despised the pleasant land,
having no faith in His promise.
They murmured in their tents,
and did not obey the voice of the Lord.
Therefore He raised His hand and swore to them
that He would make them fall in the wilderness,
and would make their offspring fall
among the nations,
scattering them among the lands. (ESV)

Deuteronomy 8: 2 - 6

Remember how the Lord your God led you all the way in the wilderness these forty years, to humble and test you in order to know what was in your heart, whether or not you would keep His commands. He humbled you, causing you to hunger and then feeding you with manna, which neither you nor your ancestors had known, to teach you that man does not live on bread alone but on every word that comes from the mouth of the Lord. Your clothes did not wear out and your feet did not swell during these forty years. Know then in your heart that as a man disciplines his son, so the Lord your God disciplines you. Observe the commands of the Lord your God, walking in obedience to Him and revering Him. (NIV)

MICAH 6: 6 - 8

With what shall I come before the Lord and bow down before the exalted God? Shall I come before Him with burnt offerings, with calves a year old? Will the Lord be pleased with thousands of rams, with ten thousand rivers of olive oil? Shall I offer my firstborn for my transgression, the fruit of my body for the sin of my soul? He has shown you, O mortal, what is good. And what does the Lord require of you? To act justly and to love mercy and to walk humbly with your God. (NIV)

PRAYER FOCUS:

Lord, I come before You in repentance for my willfulness in wanting to do things my way instead of fully listening and obeying Your ways. Show me daily how I can follow You more fully; how to be humble and merciful. Help me to revere You and walk in obedience this day, and each succeeding day, with the guidance of Your Holy Spirit living in me. Forgive me for my shortcomings as a witness for You, and give me strength each day to walk according to Your Word and be a witness for You among my family, friends and colleagues.

Av Day 15

Simeon was known for his violence. Unfortunately, this is not the best trait. For instance, he and his brother Levi were the ones who killed all the men of Shechem after convincing them to be circumcised. The story happened after their sister Dinah had been raped, and it was their way of exacting revenge instead of letting God handle it. This caused trouble for their father's household, and they had to flee for their lives.

SCRIPTURE:

Genesis 34: 13 - 30

The sons of Jacob answered Shechem and his father Hamor deceitfully, because he had defiled their sister Dinah. They said to them, "We cannot do this thing, to give our sister to one who is uncircumcised, for that would be a disgrace to us. Only on this condition will we agree with you - that you will become as we are by every male among you being circumcised. Then we will give our daughters to you, and we will take your daughters to ourselves, and we will dwell with you and become one people. But if you will not listen to us and be circumcised, then we will take our daughter, and we will be gone."

Their words pleased Hamor and Hamor's son Shechem. And the young man did not delay to do the thing, because he delighted in Jacob's daughter. Now he was the most honoured of all his father's house. So Hamor and his son Shechem came to the gate of their city and spoke to the men of their city, saying, "These men are at peace with us; let them dwell in the land and trade in it, for behold, the land is large enough for them. Let us take their daughters as wives, and let us give them our daughters. Only on this condition will the men agree to dwell with us to become one people - when every male among us is circumcised as they are circumcised. Will not their livestock, their property and all their beasts be ours? Only let us agree with them, and they will dwell with us." And all who went out of the gate of his city listened to Hamor and his son Shechem, and every male was circumcised, all who went out of the gate of his city.

On the third day, when they were sore, two of the sons of Jacob, Simeon and Levi, Dinah's brothers, took their swords and came against the city while it felt secure and killed all the males. They killed Hamor and his son Shechem with the sword and took Dinah out of Shechem's house and went away. The sons of Jacob came upon the slain and plundered the city, because they had defiled their sister. They took their flocks and their herds, their donkeys, and whatever was in the city and in the field. All their wealth, all their little ones and their wives, all that was in the houses, they captured and plundered.

Then Jacob said to Simeon and Levi, "You have brought trouble on me by making me stink to the inhabitants of the land, the Canaanites and the Perizzites. My numbers are few, and if they gather themselves against me and attack me, I shall be destroyed, both I and my household." (ESV)

Romans 12: 19
Do not take revenge, my dear friends, but leave room

for God's wrath, for it is written: "It is mine to avenge; I will repay," says the Lord. (NIV)

MATTHEW 5: 39

But I tell you, do not resist an evil person. If anyone slaps you on the right cheek, turn to them the other cheek also. (NIV)

PRAYER FOCUS:

Lord, I give every situation I find myself in to You, for Your ways are just and good. Even when I feel like I am justified in being angry or taking revenge, I pray that You would give me a heart of humility and repentance before You, that I would allow You to work out all things according to Your purposes. Your Word says You will repay. It is not my place to take revenge on those who might be persecuting me or who have dealt slanderously with me. Instead, I choose to turn the other cheek, as Jesus did, allowing You to do Your work by the Holy Spirit.

Av Day 16

When Jacob blessed his sons, he brought up the incident at Shechem and decreed that Simeon and Levi would be scattered among the other tribes. This came true for both tribes. The descendants of Levi became priests, keepers of the tabernacle, and had other holy responsibilities. Thus they were scattered among the other tribes. Simeon's tribe also received their inheritance within the boundaries of another. It is a reminder once again that our actions have consequences.

SCRIPTURE:

Genesis 49: 5 - 7 (Jacob's blessing)
"Simeon and Levi are brothers;
weapons of violence are their swords.
Let my soul come not into their council;
O my glory, be not joined to their company.
For in their anger they killed men,
and in their willfulness they hamstrung oxen.
Cursed be their anger, for it is fierce,
and their wrath, for it is cruel!
I will divide them in Jacob
and scatter them in Israel. (ESV)

JOSHUA 19: 1 and 9

The second lot came out for Simeon, for the tribe of the people of Simeon, according to their clans, and their inheritance was in the midst of the inheritance of the people of Judah...

The inheritance of the people of Simeon formed part of the territory of the people of Judah. Because the portion of the people of Judah was too large for them, the people of Simeon obtained an inheritance in the midst of their inheritance. (ESV)

PRAYER FOCUS:

Lord, again I come before You in repentance, realizing that I am a sinner and in need of Your saving grace. I also realize that my actions have consequences. Help me to accept everything that You have deemed appropriate for my life and show me how I can redeem the areas of my life where I have fallen short. I pray for divine contentment with my lot and pray for a heart that seeks after You. As You continue to reveal destructive habits to me, replace them with new, life giving habits. Show me, specifically, where I can make improvements in these areas, in Jesus name.

Av Day 17

Simeon was not the best example, but there is still a redemptive power at work this month. He was grafted in simply by his birth. As Christians, we are also grafted in by Jesus' blood and declaration, not by our own merit. God is always able to deliver us, but we must choose to follow His ways and walk in His freedom.

Scripture:

Romans 11: 22 - 32

Consider therefore the kindness and sternness of God: sternness to those who fell, but kindness to you, provided that you continue in His kindness. Otherwise, you also will be cut off. And if they do not persist in unbelief, they will be grafted in, for God is able to graft them in again. After all, if you were cut out of an olive tree that is wild by nature, and contrary to nature were grafted into a cultivated olive tree, how much more readily will these, the natural branches, be grafted into their own olive tree!

I do not want you to be ignorant of this mystery, brothers and sisters, so that you may not be conceited: Israel has experienced a hardening in part until the full number of the Gentiles has come in, and in this way all Israel will be saved. As it is written:

"The deliverer will come from Zion; He will turn godlessness away from Jacob. And this is my covenant with them when I take away their sins."

As far as the gospel is concerned, they are enemies for your sake; but as far as election is concerned, they are loved on account of the patriarchs, for God's gifts and His call are irrevocable. Just as you who were at one time disobedient to God have now received mercy as a result of their disobedience, so they too have now become disobedient in order that they too may now receive mercy as a result of God's mercy to you. For God has bound everyone over to disobedience so that He may have mercy on them all. (NIV)

PRAYER FOCUS:

Thank You that it is never too late! Even the vilest sinner can still find redemption in You, Jesus—our great and mighty Saviour! Help me to continue to choose what is right; show me when I need to humble myself and repent. Keep me steadfast in birthing and maintaining new habits as the old ones are cast away. May I be always mindful of the fact that I am grafted in, and although I have every right as a child of God, I also must never gloat or get puffed up. I lift up Your chosen people, the Jewish race and nation of Israel, and ask that You would bless them and bring them back into the fold, as You have promised, so that prophecy may be fulfilled and that the end of the age may come.

Av Day 18

We must be aware that Satan wants us to fail and will stop at nothing to see our destruction and failure. We must take steps over every root of iniquity and bitterness as quickly as possible through the Word, through praise, and through prayer.

SCRIPTURE:

1 Peter 5: 8

Be sober-minded; be watchful. Your adversary the devil prowls around like a roaring lion, seeking someone to devour. (ESV)

HEBREWS 12: 15

See to it that no one fails to obtain the grace of God; that no "root of bitterness" springs up and causes trouble, and by it many become defiled. (ESV)

PROVERBS 15:8

The sacrifice of the wicked is an abomination to the Lord, but the prayer of the upright is acceptable to Him. (ESV)

JAMES 4:7

Submit yourselves therefore to God. Resist the devil, and he will flee from you. (ESV)

. . .

Lord, You set the example for us when You quoted scripture when tempted in the wilderness. Help me to memorize Your word so that I may use it as the mighty weapon that it is when tempted by the devil or when facing his evil schemes. May hiding Your Word in my heart become a lifelong habit. Thank You that You are already showing me how to use praise and prayer as powerful weapons. Surround me with Your presence that I may be able to resist the devil and his schemes, in the mighty name of Jesus Christ, the Son of the living God!

Av Day 19

When the brothers were plotting to kill Joseph, the only one in opposition was Reuben. Likely, Simeon was in favour of the plan and was active in carrying it out. Years later when the sons of Israel went to Egypt to buy grain, Simeon is singled out to serve in prison while the rest of the family went back to Canaan. Once again, we see that poor choices have consequences.

SCRIPTURE:

Genesis 42: 24

He (Joseph) turned away from them and began to weep, but then came back and spoke to them again. He had Simeon taken from them and bound before their eyes. (NIV)

ROMANS 3: 23

For all have sinned and fall short of the glory of God. (NIV)

ROMANS 6: 20 - 23

When you were slaves to sin, you were free from the control of righteousness. What benefit did you reap at that time from the things you are now ashamed of? Those things result in death! But now that you have been set free from sin and have become slaves of God, the benefit you reap leads to holiness, and the result is eternal life. For the

wages of sin is death, but the gift of God is eternal life in
Christ Jesus our Lord. (NIV)

PRAYER FOCUS:

Thank You for Your forgiving grace and mercy! Lead
me in making good choices as I move forward and help me
to accept the things I cannot change. You are doing a great
metamorphosis this month in my life, and I embrace it
fully, knowing that in Your perfect timing, all things will
work out according to Your will and purpose. I continue to
lift up, specifically, those things that You are revealing to
me by the Holy Spirit and ask for Your continued protection and guidance.

Av Day 20

As we saw last month, Simeon camped and marched with the second group of tribes along with Reuben and Gad. Together these three tribes correspond with the summer months. Sometimes we equate the summer with laziness or inactivity—a time for taking a vacation or a holiday. While these may be rewarding and even deserved, we do not want to become lazy in doing good and following God's example.

SCRIPTURE:

Proverbs 26: 1

Like snow in summer or rain in harvest, honour is not fitting for a fool. (NIV)

PROVERBS 10: 4 - 5

A slack hand causes poverty, but the hand of the diligent makes rich. He who gathers in summer is a prudent son, but he who sleeps in harvest is a son who brings shame. (ESV)

PROVERBS 19: 15

Laziness brings on deep sleep, and the shiftless go hungry. (NIV)

GALATIANS 6: 9

Let us not become weary in doing good, for at the

proper time we will reap a harvest if we do not give up. (NIV)

2 TIMOTHY 4: 2

Preach the word; be prepared in season and out of season; correct, rebuke and encourage - with great patience and careful instruction. (NIV)

PRAYER FOCUS:

Teach me Your ways in both summer and winter; springtime and harvest. I want to follow You in every season, Lord. Forgive me for the times I have become 'slack' in my devotional time with You or in standing up for what I believe. These old patterns are banished, and I embrace a new season of fullness in You. Help me to always be ready to give an answer for my beliefs, in season and out.

Av Day 21

Zimri, a Simeonite, is mentioned as committing sexual sin with a Midianite woman in Numbers 25. Again we see negative and violent characteristics coming forward. However, as noted earlier, once we recognize these traits, we can break the iniquitous patterns in our lives by exposing them and declaring them inoperative and impotent because of the shed blood of Jesus.

SCRIPTURE:

Numbers 25: 6 - 14

Then an Israelite man brought into the camp a Midianite woman right before the eyes of Moses and the whole assembly of Israel while they were weeping at the entrance to the tent of meeting. When Phinehas son of Eleazar, the son of Aaron, the priest, saw this, he left the assembly, took a spear in his hand and followed the Israelite into the tent. He drove the spear into both of them, right through the Israelite man and into the woman's stomach. Then the plague against the Israelites was stopped; but those who died in the plague numbered 24,000.

The Lord said to Moses, "Phinehas son of Eleazar, the son of Aaron, the priest, has turned My anger away from the Israelites. Since he was as zealous for My honour among them as I am, I did not put an end to them in My zeal. Therefore tell him I am making My covenant of peace with him. He and his descendants will have a covenant of a lasting priesthood, because he was zealous for the honour of his God and made atonement for the Israelites."

The name of the Israelite who was killed with the Midianite woman was Zimri son of Salu, the leader of a Simeonite family. (NIV)

PRAYER FOCUS:

Thank You for the times You have shed light on my own sin. Expose every dark place within me and make me clean before You. I realize that this is a process, and so I submit to whatever it takes, choosing faith over unbelief as I surrender to Your will. I choose life today, in Jesus name.

Av Day 22

The tribe of Simeon fought alongside Judah to help them take their inheritance, and then Judah returned the favour. Eventually, Simeon was given territory within the borders of Judah, fulfilling the prophecy of the patriarch Jacob when he said they would be scattered among their brothers. However, we do see the positive characteristic of loyalty and strength in this scenario since they came alongside and helped their brother Judah, as promised. The tribe of Simeon turned out to be people of their word.

SCRIPTURE:

Psalm 41: 11 - 12

By this I know that You delight in me: my enemy will not shout in triumph over me.

But You have upheld me because of my integrity, and set me in Your presence forever. (ESV)

1 TIMOTHY 1: 18 - 19

Timothy, my son, I am giving you this command in keeping with the prophecies once made about you, so that by recalling them you may fight the battle well, holding on to faith and a good conscience, which some have rejected and so have suffered shipwreck with regard to the faith. (NIV)

PROVERBS 25: 13

Like a snow-cooled drink at harvest time is a trustworthy messenger to the one who sends him; he refreshes the spirit of his master. (NIV)

PRAYER FOCUS:

Lord, I want to be known as a person of my word. Show me how I can demonstrate integrity each and every day as I walk with You. Thank You for the many examples of faithful men and women given in Your Word. Point me to those passages that You would have me meditate on today, and help me to apply them to my own life and to the lives of those I love as I pray for them and for the church as a whole.

Av Day 23

Over 7000 warriors from Simeon came to join David at Hebron when he was anointed King. Again we see the positive characteristics mentioned yesterday. It goes to show that despite the possible negatives, God can still use anyone—a relief, since who among us is without sin?

SCRIPTURE:

1 Chronicles 12: 23 and 25

These are the numbers of the men armed for battle who came to David at Hebron to turn Saul's kingdom over to him, as the Lord had said... from Simeon, warriors ready for battle - 7,100. (NIV)

1 TIMOTHY 1: 12 - 17

I thank Christ Jesus our Lord, who has given me strength, that He considered me trustworthy, appointing me to His service. Even though I was once a blasphemer and a persecutor and a violent man, I was shown mercy because I acted in ignorance and unbelief. The grace of our Lord was poured out on me abundantly, along with the faith and love that are in Christ Jesus.

Here is a trustworthy saying that deserves full acceptance: Christ Jesus came into the world to save sinners - of whom I am the worst. But for that very reason I was shown mercy so that in me, the worst of sinners, Christ Jesus might display His immense patience as an example for those who would believe in Him and receive eternal

life. Now to the King eternal, immortal, invisible, the only
God, be honour and glory for ever and ever. Amen. (NIV)

PRAYER FOCUS:

Like Paul, I am a chief among sinners! Yet You have
shown me such great mercy, Lord—a mercy that I do not
deserve, but that was freely given anyway. May I go
forward in battle for You as a trustworthy warrior,
strengthened by Your mighty hand.

Av Day 24

Moses did not give a blessing or any prophetic word over Simeon when he blessed the other tribes in Deuteronomy 33 before his death. They are the only tribe left out. It serves as a sobering reminder that there are consequences to sin. Even though God's grace is abundant, we may still need to pay for our actions. As well, we must never become complacent in our faith. In the New Testament, a man named Simon thought he could use the gifts for his own gain, even though he was already a believer. This is another reminder that even if we are saved we should check our motives daily.

SCRIPTURE:

Acts 3: 19

Repent, then, and turn to God, so that your sins may be wiped out, that times of refreshing may come from the Lord. (NIV)

ACTS 8: 9 - 24

Now for some time a man named Simon had practiced sorcery in the city and amazed all the people of Samaria. He boasted that he was someone great, and all the people, both high and low, gave him their attention and exclaimed, "This man is rightly called the Great Power of God." They followed him because he had amazed them for a long time with his sorcery. But when they believed Philip as he proclaimed the good news of the kingdom of

God and the name of Jesus Christ, they were baptized, both men and women. Simon himself believed and was baptized. And he followed Philip everywhere, astonished by the great signs and miracles he saw.

When the apostles in Jerusalem heard that Samaria had accepted the word of God, they sent Peter and John to Samaria. When they arrived, they prayed for the new believers there that they might receive the Holy Spirit, because the Holy Spirit had not yet come on any of them; they had simply been baptized in the name of the Lord Jesus. Then Peter and John placed their hands on them, and they received the Holy Spirit. When Simon saw that the Spirit was given at the laying on of the apostles' hands, he offered them money and said, "Give me also this ability so that everyone on whom I lay my hands may receive the Holy Spirit."

Peter answered: "May your money perish with you, because you thought you could buy the gift of God with money! You have no part or share in this ministry, because your heart is not right before God. Repent of this wickedness and pray to the Lord in the hope that He may forgive you for having such a thought in your heart. For I see that you are full of bitterness and captive to sin."

Then Simon answered, "Pray to the Lord for me so that nothing you have said may happen to me." (NIV)

PRAYER FOCUS:

Search my heart and reveal to me any impure motives that I may be carrying. Cleanse me so that I may be used of You and that I may use the gifts of the Spirit as You see fit—not as I see fit. Give me patience when I must still endure the consequences of my own actions, and help me to always look to You and the greater good—in Jesus name.

Av Day 25

Even though Moses did not bless the tribe of Simeon, Ezekiel includes them in the tribes who will inhabit territory in the coming kingdom. They are positioned at the South Gate along with Issachar and Zebulun, which is a change from their positioning during the time of Moses and Joshua. Again, we see that with God's redemptive power, it is never too late! He has a plan and a purpose for each and every individual on earth.

Scripture:

Ezekiel 48: 24 and 33

"Simeon will have one portion; it will border the territory of Benjamin from east to west."...

"On the south side, which measures 4,500 cubits, will be three gates: the gate of Simeon, the gate of Issachar and the gate of Zebulun." (NIV)

Jeremiah 29: 10 - 14

This is what the Lord says: "When seventy years are completed for Babylon, I will come to you and fulfill my good promise to bring you back to this place. For I know the plans I have for you," declares the Lord, "plans to prosper you and not to harm you, plans to give you hope and a future. Then you will call on Me and come and pray to Me, and I will listen to you. You will seek Me and find Me when you seek Me with all your heart. I will be found by you," declares the Lord, "and will bring you back from captivity. I will gather you from all the nations and places where I have banished you," declares the Lord, "and will bring you back to the place from which I carried you into exile." (NIV)

NEHEMIAH 9: 17b

But You are a forgiving God, gracious and compassionate, slow to anger and abounding in love. (NIV)

PRAYER FOCUS:

Thank You that You have a plan and purpose for my life. Help me to never forget that. In times of doubt or despair, bring to mind Your Words of hope and truth, for You are a God of mercy—slow to anger and abounding in love. Thank You for the mighty work You are doing in my life and will continue to do as I remain steadfast in following You.

Av Day 26

The month of Av contains many lessons—some of them quite difficult. The good thing about landing at the very bottom, however, is that there is only one way out— up! God graciously allows us to learn from our mistakes. While we are urged to make right choices, He never forces good upon us. In the end, His ways are always righteous and just.

SCRIPTURE:

James 1: 9 - 15

Believers in humble circumstances ought to take pride in their high position. But the rich should take pride in their humiliation - since they will pass away like a wild flower. For the sun rises with scorching heat and withers the plant; its blossom falls and its beauty is destroyed. In the same way, the rich will fade away even while they go about their business.

Blessed is the one who perseveres under trial because, having stood the test, that person will receive the crown of life that the Lord has promised to those who love him.

When tempted, no one should say, "God is tempting me." For God cannot be tempted by evil, nor does He tempt anyone; but each person is tempted when they are dragged away by their own evil desire and enticed. Then, after desire has conceived, it gives birth to sin; and sin, when it is full-grown, gives birth to death.

(NIV)

.   .   .

ROMANS 5:12 to 6:2

Therefore, just as sin came into the world through one man, and death through sin, and so death spread to all men because all sinned - for sin indeed was in the world before the law was given, but sin is not counted where there is no law. Yet death reigned from Adam to Moses, even over those whose sinning was not like the transgression of Adam, who was a type of the one who was to come.

But the free gift is not like the trespass. For if many died through one man's trespass, much more have the grace of God and the free gift by the grace of that one man Jesus Christ abounded for many. And the free gift is not like the result of that one man's sin. For the judgment following one trespass brought condemnation, but the free gift following many trespasses brought justification. For if, because of one man's trespass, death reigned through that one man, much more will those who receive the abundance of grace and the free gift of righteousness reign in life through the one man Jesus Christ.

Therefore, as one trespass led to condemnation for all men, so one act of righteousness leads to justification and life for all men. For as by the one man's disobedience the many were made sinners, so by the one man's obedience the many will be made righteous. Now the law came in to increase the trespass, but where sin increased, grace abounded all the more, so that, as sin reigned in death, grace also might reign through righteousness leading to eternal life through Jesus Christ our Lord.

What shall we say then? Are we to continue in sin that grace may abound? By no means! How can we who died to sin still live in it? (ESV)

. . .

PRAYER FOCUS:

Thank You that You are gracious and compassionate, allowing me to learn from my mistakes, and now, because of the new covenant in Jesus' blood, I am redeemed. Help me to walk each day in the newness of life You have given me. Continue to reveal to me Your plan and purpose for my life. Remind me of those things I must continue to release to You such as any iniquitous patterns that I may still struggle with. Thank You for the new, life giving habits You are cementing in me so that I may be a worthy member of the army of God.

Av Day 27

We all need discernment, and as we move forward toward the next month, it is even more imperative that we get in tune with the Holy Spirit. As we watch our alignments, we must not resist the leading of the Lord.

SCRIPTURE:

Psalm 49
Hear this, all you peoples;
listen, all who live in this world,
both low and high,
rich and poor alike:
My mouth will speak words of wisdom;
the meditation of my heart
will give you understanding.
I will turn my ear to a proverb;
with the harp I will expound my riddle:
Why should I fear when evil days come,
when wicked deceivers surround me -
those who trust in their wealth
and boast of their great riches?
No one can redeem the life of another
or give to God a ransom for them -
the ransom for a life is costly,
no payment is ever enough -
so that they should live on forever
and not see decay.
For all can see that the wise die,
that the foolish and the senseless also perish,
leaving their wealth to others.

Their tombs will remain their houses forever,
their dwellings for endless generations,
though they had named lands after themselves.
People, despite their wealth, do not endure;
they are like the beasts that perish.
This is the fate of those who trust in themselves,
and of their followers, who approve their sayings.
They are like sheep and are destined to die;
death will be their shepherd
(but the upright will prevail over them in the morning).
Their forms will decay in the grave,
far from their princely mansions.
But God will redeem me from the realm of the dead;
He will surely take me to Himself.
Do not be overawed when others grow rich,
when the splendour of their houses increases;
for they will take nothing with them when they die,
their splendour will not descend with them.
Though while they live they count themselves blessed
and people praise you when you prosper.
They will join those who have gone before them,
who will never again see the light of life.
People who have wealth but lack understanding
are like the beasts that perish. (NIV)

PROVERBS 10:14

Wise people treasure knowledge, but the babbling of a
fool invites disaster. (NLT)

. . .

PRAYER FOCUS:

Forgive me for the times when I decided I 'knew better' and didn't listen to wise counsel. Instead, help me to 'tune in' to what You are saying and to listen to the wise counsel of others You have put in my life. Give me discernment beyond my own abilities, in Jesus name.

Av Day 28

Despite what we may have been through this month, or even in our lives in general, God has never left our side. He will never leave us or forsake us, for He is the God of all comfort. Like a woman in childbirth, we must rest in the knowledge that our trials will result in great joy and will be used by God for His purposes.

Scripture:

2 Corinthians 1: 3 - 7

Blessed be the God and Father of our Lord Jesus Christ, the Father of mercies and God of all comfort, who comforts us in all our affliction, so that we may be able to comfort those who are in any affliction, with the comfort with which we ourselves are comforted by God. For as we share abundantly in Christ's sufferings, so through Christ we share abundantly in comfort too. If we are afflicted, it is for your comfort and salvation; and if we are comforted, it is for your comfort, which you experience when you patiently endure the same sufferings that we suffer. Our hope for you is unshaken, for we know that as you share in our sufferings, you will also share in our comfort. (ESV)

Isaiah 40: 1 - 5

Comfort, comfort my people, says your God.
Speak tenderly to Jerusalem,
and cry to her that her warfare is ended,
that her iniquity is pardoned,
that she has received from the Lord's hand

double for all her sins.
A voice cries:
"In the wilderness prepare the way of the Lord;
make straight in the desert a highway for our God.
Every valley shall be lifted up,
and every mountain and hill be made low;
the uneven ground shall become level,
and the rough places a plain.
And the glory of the Lord shall be revealed,
and all flesh shall see it together,
for the mouth of the Lord has spoken." (ESV)

Psalm 48

Great is the Lord, and most worthy of praise,
in the city of our God, His holy mountain.
Beautiful in its loftiness,
the joy of the whole earth,
like the heights of Zaphon is Mount Zion,
the city of the Great King.
God is in her citadels;
He has shown Himself to be her fortress.
When the kings joined forces,
when they advanced together,
they saw her and were astounded;
they fled in terror.
Trembling seized them there,
pain like that of a woman in labor.
You destroyed them like ships of Tarshish
shattered by an east wind.
As we have heard,

so we have seen
in the city of the Lord Almighty,
in the city of our God:
God makes her secure forever.
Within Your temple, O God,
we meditate on Your unfailing love.
Like Your name, O God,
Your praise reaches to the ends of the earth;
Your right hand is filled with righteousness.
Mount Zion rejoices,
the villages of Judah are glad
because of Your judgments.
Walk about Zion, go around her,
count her towers,
consider well her ramparts,
view her citadels,
that you may tell of them
to the next generation.
For this God is our God for ever and ever;
He will be our guide even to the end. (NIV)

DEUTERONOMY 31: 8

The Lord Himself goes before you and will be with you; He will never leave you nor forsake you. Do not be afraid; do not be discouraged. (NIV)

PRAYER FOCUS:

Thank You for Your great mercy and comfort to all those who believe. Surround me with Your compassion and care that I may show compassion to others. Thank You that You have never left my side. I surrender to Your comfort and healing today. Strengthen me for the battles and disappointments that are still to come in my life, and help me to use what I have learned to minister to others who may also be going through difficult circumstances.

Av Day 29

As we weave the Word, praise and prayer into our lives, we are able to stand firm no matter what may come our way. We know that ultimately God has a plan and purpose for our lives and that in the end, the victory is His. However, it is up to us to break away from old patterns of iniquity and follow God's plan instead.

Scripture:

Romans 4: 7 - 17

"Blessed are those whose transgressions are forgiven, whose sins are covered. Blessed is the one whose sin the Lord will never count against them."

Is this blessedness only for the circumcised, or also for the uncircumcised? We have been saying that Abraham's faith was credited to him as righteousness. Under what circumstances was it credited? Was it after he was circumcised, or before? It was not after, but before! And he received circumcision as a sign, a seal of the righteousness that he had by faith while he was still uncircumcised. So then, he is the father of all who believe but have not been circumcised, in order that righteousness might be credited to them. And he is then also the father of the circumcised who not only are circumcised but who also follow in the footsteps of the faith that our father Abraham had before he was circumcised.

It was not through the law that Abraham and his offspring received the promise that he would be heir of the world, but through the righteousness that comes by faith. For if those who depend on the law are heirs, faith means

nothing and the promise is worthless, because the law
brings wrath. And where there is no law there is no transgression.

Therefore, the promise comes by faith, so that it may
be by grace and may be guaranteed to all Abraham's
offspring - not only to those who are of the law but also to
those who have the faith of Abraham. He is the father of
us all. As it is written: "I have made you a father of many
nations." He is our father in the sight of God, in whom he
believed - the God who gives life to the dead and calls into
being things that were not. (NIV)

Psalm 32
    Blessed is the one whose transgressions are forgiven,
    whose sins are covered.
    Blessed is the one whose sin
    the Lord does not count against them
    and in whose spirit is no deceit.
    When I kept silent, my bones wasted away
    through my groaning all day long.
    For day and night Your hand was heavy on me;
    my strength was sapped as in the heat of summer.
    Then I acknowledged my sin to You
    and did not cover up my iniquity.
    I said, "I will confess my transgressions to the Lord."
    And You forgave the guilt of my sin.
    Therefore let all the faithful pray to You
    while You may be found;
    surely the rising of the mighty waters
    will not reach them.

You are my hiding place;
You will protect me from trouble
and surround me with songs of deliverance.
I will instruct you and teach you
in the way you should go;
I will counsel you with my loving eye on you.
Do not be like the horse or the mule,
which have no understanding
but must be controlled by bit and bridle
or they will not come to you.
Many are the woes of the wicked,
but the Lord's unfailing love
surrounds the one who trusts in Him.
Rejoice in the Lord and be glad, you righteous;
sing, all you who are upright in heart! (NIV)

PRAYER FOCUS:

I rejoice before You today, Oh Lord, and magnify Your wonderful name! I praise You for You made me in my mother's womb, and every day was set out for me before the beginning of time. Search my heart to see if there is any unrighteous thing in me, that I might confess all to You. Cleanse me, teach me, guide me—in Jesus name. Amen.

Av Day 30

We've seen that the month of Av is often considered the low month in the Hebrew calendar, but thankfully, it can be restored as a month of blessing, as God originally intended. We can exchange mourning for dancing and sorrow for joy. Praise Him today for His infinite mercy and goodness!

SCRIPTURE:

Zechariah 7: 2 - 10

Now the people of Bethel had sent Sharezer and Regem-melech and their men to entreat the favor of the Lord, saying to the priests of the house of the Lord of hosts and the prophets, "Should I weep and abstain in the fifth month, as I have done for so many years?"

Then the word of the Lord of hosts came to me: "Say to all the people of the land and the priests, 'When you fasted and mourned in the fifth month and in the seventh, for these seventy years, was it for me that you fasted? And when you eat and when you drink, do you not eat for yourselves and drink for yourselves? Were not these the words that the Lord proclaimed by the former prophets, when Jerusalem was inhabited and prosperous, with her cities around her, and the South and the lowland were inhabited?'"

And the word of the Lord came to Zechariah, saying, "Thus says the Lord of hosts, render true judgments, show kindness and mercy to one another, do not oppress the widow, the fatherless, the sojourner, or the poor, and let none of you devise evil against another in your heart." (ESV)

Psalm 145: 8

The Lord is gracious and compassionate, slow to anger and rich in love. (NIV)

Isaiah 61: 3

To appoint unto them that mourn in Zion, to give unto them beauty for ashes, the oil of joy for mourning, the garment of praise for the spirit of heaviness; that they might be called trees of righteousness, the planting of the Lord, that He might be glorified. (KJV)

Psalm 8

Lord, our Lord,
how majestic is Your name in all the earth!
You have set Your glory in the heavens.
Through the praise of children and infants
You have established a stronghold
against Your enemies,
to silence the foe and the avenger.
When I consider Your heavens,
the work of Your fingers,
the moon and the stars, which You have set in place,
what is mankind that You are mindful of them,
human beings that You care for them?
You have made them a little lower than the angels

and crowned them with glory and honour.
You made them rulers over the works of Your hands;
You put everything under their feet:
all flocks and herds, and the animals of the wild,
the birds in the sky, and the fish in the sea,
all that swim the paths of the seas.
Lord, our Lord,
how majestic is Your name in all the earth! (NIV)

PRAYER FOCUS:

I praise You for who You are. You deserve all praise, honour and glory, and I worship You today. As I prepare to move forward into the next month, instill in me a wonder of Your greatness and an awe of You. May the lessons learned this month never be far from my mind and spirit. Amen.

E

LUL - Month 6
The Month of Gad
29 days - August/September

THIS IS the sixth month of the Hebrew year and the third month of summer. We are now on an upward trajectory toward the holy days of the seventh mont— a time set apart as special. As we prepare, God continues to teach us lessons about relying on Him, and Him alone, surrendering all to Him so that we can experience His fullness.

Elul Day 1 - Rosh Chodesh

Abraham's willingness to sacrifice his son Isaac was a type of firstfruits offering. Isaac represented God's promise to Abraham, yet Abraham was willing to give Isaac up because he believed God had a plan and could do a miracle if necessary. Think about what you are willing to give up in order to obey God. He wants each one of us to prepare our hearts to meet with Him in a special way next month, and this is the beginning of that process.

Scripture:

Genesis 17: 19

God said, "No, but Sarah your wife shall bear you a son, and you shall call his name Isaac. I will establish my covenant with him as an everlasting covenant for his offspring after him. (ESV)

Genesis 22: 1 - 18

After these things God tested Abraham and said to him, "Abraham!" And he said, "Here I am." He said, "Take your son, your only son Isaac, whom you love, and go to the land of Moriah, and offer him there as a burnt offering on one of the mountains of which I shall tell you." So Abraham rose early in the morning, saddled his donkey, and took two of his young men with him, and his son Isaac. And he cut the wood for the burnt offering and arose and went to the place of which God had told him. On the third day Abraham lifted up his eyes and saw the place from afar. Then Abraham said to his young men,

"Stay here with the donkey; I and the boy will go over there and worship and come again to you." And Abraham took the wood of the burnt offering and laid it on Isaac his son. And he took in his hand the fire and the knife. So they went both of them together. And Isaac said to his father Abraham, "My father!" And he said, "Here I am, my son." He said, "Behold, the fire and the wood, but where is the lamb for a burnt offering?" Abraham said, "God will provide for Himself the lamb for a burnt offering, my son." So they went both of them together.

When they came to the place of which God had told him, Abraham built the altar there and laid the wood in order and bound Isaac his son and laid him on the altar, on top of the wood. Then Abraham reached out his hand and took the knife to slaughter his son. But the angel of the Lord called to him from heaven and said, "Abraham, Abraham!" And he said, "Here I am." He said, "Do not lay your hand on the boy or do anything to him, for now I know that you fear God, seeing you have not withheld your son, your only son, from me." And Abraham lifted up his eyes and looked, and behold, behind him was a ram, caught in a thicket by his horns. And Abraham went and took the ram and offered it up as a burnt offering instead of his son. So Abraham called the name of that place, "The Lord will provide"; as it is said to this day, "On the mount of the Lord it shall be provided."

And the angel of the Lord called to Abraham a second time from heaven and said, "By myself I have sworn, declares the Lord, because you have done this and have not withheld your son, your only son, I will surely bless you, and I will surely multiply your offspring as the stars of heaven and as the sand that is on the seashore. And your offspring shall possess the gate of his enemies, and in your offspring shall all the nations of the earth be blessed, because you have obeyed my voice." (ESV)

Hebrews 11: 17 - 19

By faith Abraham, when God tested him, offered Isaac as a sacrifice. He who had embraced the promises was about to sacrifice his one and only son, even though God had said to him, "It is through Isaac that your offspring will be reckoned." Abraham reasoned that God could even raise the dead, and so in a manner of speaking he did receive Isaac back from death. (NIV)

Prayer focus:

I praise You, today, Lord! You are a God of covenant and I thank You that I can trust You with everything—even that which is most precious to me. I thank You that You always make a way. Your plans and Your ways are so much higher than mine. Help me to surrender to You in everything, even in those things which may seem hard or impossible. Enable me as I purpose to give You the firstfruits of my time and the best of my day. I just want to dwell in Your presence this month. Meet with me one on one as I rest in You and prepare my heart for the coming holy days in the next month. You are my fortress and my deliverer and I praise You, in Jesus name.

Elul Day 2

As already discussed, each month of the Hebrew calendar corresponds with a letter of the alphabet, which in turn is found in Psalm 119, David's acrostic celebrating God's Word. The month of Elul is represented by the letter YUD, YODH or YOD, which means 'appointed mercy from the hand of God'. God has stretched out His hand toward us and in His great mercy, provided a way for our salvation.

Scripture:

Psalm 119: 73 - 80
Your hands have made and fashioned me;
give me understanding
that I may learn Your commandments.
Those who fear You shall see me and rejoice,
because I have hoped in Your word.
I know, O Lord, that Your rules are righteous,
and that in faithfulness You have afflicted me.
Let Your steadfast love comfort me
according to Your promise to Your servant.
Let Your mercy come to me, that I may live;
for Your law is my delight.
Let the insolent be put to shame,
because they have wronged me with falsehood;
as for me, I will meditate on Your precepts.
Let those who fear You turn to me,
that they may know Your testimonies.
May my heart be blameless in Your statutes,
that I may not be put to shame! (ESV)

·   ·   ·

PRAYER FOCUS:

You have showered Your mercy on me already in that I,
the chief of sinners, was chosen to be grafted into Your
family. In Your mercy, reach down and touch the lives of
all my loved ones who do not yet know You or who have
not surrendered to You. I pray that my entire family will
one day gather before Your throne, united and together.

Elul Day 3

Elul represents the third month of summer. It is associated with a Jewish tradition where the king would leave his palace and move to a tent in a field near the city. I'm sure the tent was more than a piece of canvas, but it showed good will toward the people in that it was a time of special accessibility. Criers would announce, "The King is in the field!" which meant that commoners could approach him with their concerns rather than having to go through the normal—and sometimes difficult—protocols that were expected. In effect, he dwelt among them. Similarly, God came to earth in the flesh and dwelt among us for a season. Through Jesus, God is accessible and available to all who believe. Expect Him to meet with you this month in your everyday life!

SCRIPTURE:

John 1: 14

The Word became flesh and made His dwelling among us. We have seen His glory, the glory of the one and only Son, who came from the Father, full of grace and truth. (NIV)

EPHESIANS 3: 12

In Him and through faith in Him we may approach God with freedom and confidence.

(NIV)

.   .   .

HEBREWS 4: 16

Let us then with confidence draw near to the throne of grace, that we may receive mercy and find grace to help in time of need. (ESV)

PRAYER FOCUS**:**

Thank You Lord that You have made Yourself accessible to us, bridging the chasm between God and man so that we may come boldly before You. Lord, I expect to meet with You this month in every ordinary aspect of my life. I lift up my family and my loved ones to You today, and ask for Your mercy and grace to be upon them, in Jesus name.

Elul Day 4

Moses ascended the mountain to receive the second set of tablets during this month. He had smashed the first set when he came down from the mountain and saw the golden calf, witnessing the people's grave sin as they engaged in idolatry. But God provided a second chance for the people by allowing Moses to go a second time and receive a new set of tablets. God is merciful to us and gives us more than one chance, too. He can show us the strategies we need to repair what has been broken in our lives, and if something isn't fixable, we can ask Him to show us so we can start fresh. In preparation for the 'high holy days' coming in the next month, Elul is a month to fix what has been broken.

SCRIPTURE:

Exodus 34: 1 - 9

The Lord said to Moses, "Chisel out two stone tablets like the first ones, and I will write on them the words that were on the first tablets, which you broke. Be ready in the morning, and then come up on Mount Sinai. Present yourself to me there on top of the mountain. No one is to come with you or be seen anywhere on the mountain; not even the flocks and herds may graze in front of the mountain."

So Moses chiseled out two stone tablets like the first ones and went up Mount Sinai early in the morning, as the Lord had commanded him; and he carried the two stone tablets in his hands. Then the Lord came down in the cloud and stood there with him and proclaimed His name, the Lord. And He passed in front of Moses, proclaiming, "The Lord, the Lord, the compassionate and gracious God, slow to anger, abounding in love and faithfulness, maintaining love to thousands, and forgiving wickedness, rebellion and sin. Yet He does not leave the guilty unpunished; He punishes the children and their children for the sin of the parents to the third and fourth generation."

Moses bowed to the ground at once and worshiped. "Lord," he said, "if I have found favour in Your eyes, then let the Lord go with us. Although this is a stiff-necked people, forgive our wickedness and our sin, and take us as Your inheritance." (NIV)

PRAYER FOCUS:

I bring before You today the things in my life that need fixing: relationships, finances, my physical body and the ailments of others - everything that needs to be fixed or started fresh. As I list them specifically as they come to mind, I lay each thing on the altar at Your feet, trusting that You are the great physician, able to do far above what I ask or even imagine. Forgive me for my sin! I cry out to You for my loved ones and pray that you would reveal any lingering stubbornness or iniquity so that I might bring it to You to be dealt with once and for all—in Jesus name.

Elul Day 5

The tribe of Gad camped on the south side of the tabernacle with Reuben and Simeon and also marched out with them, second in line after the first group of three comprised of Judah, Issachar and Zebulun. They knew their place and their assignment, which was to provide strong reinforcements for the people in front and a protective barrier for the Levites coming next with the holy articles. They were a necessary part of the larger community and knew their place within it. Similarly, we also need to find our place within the body of Christ and work as a unit in moving forward. We need community. We need each other. It is why we are told not to forsake assembling ourselves together, for it is in isolation that the enemy can pick us off.

Scripture:

Numbers 2: 10 - 17

On the south side shall be the standard of the camp of Reuben by their companies, the chief of the people of Reuben being Elizur the son of Shedeur, his company as listed being 46,500. And those to camp next to him shall be the tribe of Simeon, the chief of the people of Simeon being Shelumiel the son of Zurishaddai, his company as listed being 59,300. Then the tribe of Gad, the chief of the people of Gad being Eliasaph the son of Reuel, his company as listed being 45,650. All those listed of the camp of Reuben, by their companies, were 151,450. They shall set out second.

Then the tent of meeting shall set out, with the camp

of the Levites in the midst of the camps; as they camp, so shall they set out, each in position, standard by standard. (ESV)

HEBREWS 10: 23 - 25

Let us hold fast the confession of our hope without wavering, for He who promised is faithful; and let us consider how to stimulate one another to love and good deeds, not forsaking our own assembling together, as is the habit of some, but encouraging one another; and all the more as you see the day drawing near. (NASB)

PRAYER FOCUS:

Forgive me, Lord, for the times I have tried to do things in isolation. I recognize that the devil seeks out lone sheep to pick them off and I also recognize my need of the greater body and my need for fellowship. Help me to find my place within the body of Christ; to discover the gifts, talents, and skills that You have bestowed on me and to willingly do the service that You are calling me to, no matter what it is.

Elul Day 6

God wants to protect and nurture us—to provide us with a safe haven so that we can rest and regroup. This is especially important after the ravages of battle. We can run into His tower and be safe and secure. He is our city of refuge.

SCRIPTURE:

Proverbs 18: 10

The name of the Lord is a strong tower; The righteous runs into it and is safe. (NASB)

PROVERBS 14: 26

Whoever fears the Lord has a secure fortress, and for their children it will be a refuge. (NIV)

PSALM 37: 7

Rest in the Lord and wait patiently for Him; do not fret because of him who prospers in his way, because of the man who carries out wicked schemes. (NASB)

PSALM 91: 4

He will cover you with His feathers, and under His wings you will find refuge; His faithfulness will be your shield and rampart. (NIV)

.   .   .

PRAYER FOCUS:

Your name is a strong tower, Oh Lord! Blessed be Your name, Most High. I run to You, away from all the stress and strife of this world. I take shelter under Your wings. I claim refuge, for I am weak, but You are strong. You have opened Your gates and let me in; they are shut against all my enemies. Every plot, scheme, and secret plan of the enemy that is formed against me or my loved ones is exposed, for I have a great watchman, even the Lord Almighty, on the tower heights. May I rest in You and in the safety of Your haven as I regroup and regain strength for the coming days.

Elul Day 7

According to tradition, Rebekah gave birth to Jacob and Esau in this month. Because of this, it has become known as the month of nurturing, as a mother nurtures her children. This fits well with yesterday's lesson that the Lord is our safe haven—a place of refuge and rest. However, it is also a time to think about what may be trying to contend within us, even as Jacob and Esau contended with one another in Rebekah's womb. Sometimes situations can be multifaceted. There are two sides to every coin and most things cannot be placed neatly into 'black and white' boxes. As we rest in the Lord and allow Him to nurture us, it is wise to identify the areas in our lives that may be pulling us in more than one direction so that we can pray for wisdom, guidance and strength.

SCRIPTURE:

Genesis 25: 21 - 24

Isaac prayed to the Lord on behalf of his wife, because she was childless. The Lord answered his prayer, and his wife Rebekah became pregnant. The babies jostled each other within her, and she said, "Why is this happening to me?" So she went to inquire of the Lord.

The Lord said to her, "Two nations are in your womb, and two peoples from within you will be separated; one people will be stronger than the other, and the older will serve the younger."

When the time came for her to give birth, there were twin boys in her womb. The first to come out was red, and his whole body was like a hairy garment; so they named him Esau. After this, his brother came out, with his hand grasping Esau's heel; so he was named Jacob. Isaac was sixty years old when Rebekah gave birth to them. (NIV)

JAMES 4: 1

What causes fights and quarrels among you? Don't they come from your desires that battle within you? (NIV)

PROVERBS 14: 33

Wisdom reposes in the heart of the discerning and even among fools she lets herself be known. (NIV)

PRAYER FOCUS:

Thank You once again for Your nurturing. I recognize that I need Your care, Lord, and I also pray that You would help me to nurture others as You lead. As well, show me the areas in my life where there is contention or double mindedness, be it in relationships, circumstances, situations or any other area. Help me to choose the path of life in every situation, for the battles of my life are internal as well as external.

Elul Day 8

As part of our spiritual preparation, it is a timely opportunity to examine how our faith is evident in our actions. Of course, we realize that works do not equal salvation, but James exhorts us with the words that 'faith without works is dead'. In other words, true faith requires action.

SCRIPTURE:

James 2: 14 - 26

What good is it, my brothers, if someone says he has faith but does not have works? Can that faith save him? If a brother or sister is poorly clothed and lacking in daily food, and one of you says to them, "Go in peace, be warmed and filled," without giving them the things needed for the body, what good is that? So also faith by itself, if it does not have works, is dead.

But someone will say, "You have faith and I have works." Show me your faith apart from your works, and I will show you my faith by my works. You believe that God is one; you do well. Even the demons believe - and shudder! Do you want to be shown, you foolish person, that faith apart from works is useless? Was not Abraham our father justified by works when he offered up his son Isaac on the altar? You see that faith was active along with his works, and faith was completed by his works; and the Scripture was fulfilled that says, "Abraham believed God, and it was counted to him as righteousness" - and he was called a friend of God. You see that a person is justified by works and not by faith alone. And in the same way was not also Rahab the prostitute justified by works when she received the messengers and sent them out by another way? For as the body apart from the spirit is dead, so also faith apart from works is dead. (ESV)

JAMES 1: 22

But prove yourselves doers of the word, and not merely hearers who delude themselves. (NASB)

PRAYER FOCUS:

Help me to be a doer of the Word and not only a hearer. Increase my faith as I walk with You, Lord, and show me ways that I can be an active participant in the Kingdom as I prepare my heart to meet with You in a more intimate way next month.

Elul Day 9

The book of Hebrews defines faith as, "confidence in what we hope for and assurance about what we do not see." (NIV) Active faith means believing God's promises and moving forward in what He has called us to do, even when the physical realm doesn't necessarily line up. When we intercede for someone or bring a certain situation before the Lord, we must move forward after an appropriate length of time, believing that God has heard and that He has answered. We can view our intercession for certain situations as a 'project' that has a beginning and an end, not an endless plea that is never heard. That is faith in action—believing that God has heard and then moving forward.

SCRIPTURE:

Hebrews 11: 1

Now faith is the assurance of things hoped for, the conviction of things not seen. (ESV)

2 CORINTHIANS 8: 11

But now finish doing it also, so that just as there was the readiness to desire it, so there may be also the completion of it by your ability. (NASB)

ROMANS 2: 13 - 16

For it is not the hearers of the Law who are just before God, but the doers of the Law will be justified. For when

Gentiles who do not have the Law do instinctively the things of the Law, these, not having the Law, are a law to themselves, in that they show the work of the Law written in their hearts, their conscience bearing witness and their thoughts alternately accusing or else defending them, on the day when, according to my gospel, God will judge the secrets of men through Christ Jesus. (NASB)

LUKE 11:28

He replied, "Blessed rather are those who hear the word of God and obey it." (NIV)

PRAYER FOCUS:

Activate any dormant faith within me, Lord, so that I may move forward, believing that You have already accomplished what has been ordained for me and my family from the beginning of time. I want to be obedient to You and to Your Word in all things, even when my surroundings do not seem to line up with what I know and believe. I believe that You are in control of my life, that You hear my prayers, and that You are just and righteous.

Elul Day 10

Hebrews Chapter 11 is often called the 'Faith hall of fame' because it lists many Biblical characters who exhibited strong faith. We can learn a lot from these people about what faith in action means. As you read this passage, make a list of the characteristics and or actions of each person, then pray about how to implement these same things in your own life. For further understanding, find each story in the Old Testament and study each person's life more closely to find out why they were included in this line up of faithful all-stars.

Scripture:

Hebrews 11

Now faith is confidence in what we hope for and assurance about what we do not see. This is what the ancients were commended for.

By faith we understand that the universe was formed at God's command, so that what is seen was not made out of what was visible.

By faith Abel brought God a better offering than Cain did. By faith he was commended as righteous, when God spoke well of his offerings. And by faith Abel still speaks, even though he is dead.

By faith Enoch was taken from this life, so that he did not experience death: "He could not be found, because God had taken him away." For before he was taken, he was commended as one who pleased God. And without faith it is impossible to please God, because anyone who comes to him must believe that he exists and that he rewards those who earnestly seek him.

By faith Noah, when warned about things not yet seen, in holy fear built an ark to save his family. By his faith he condemned the world and became heir of the righteousness that is in keeping with faith.

By faith Abraham, when called to go to a place he would later receive as his inheritance, obeyed and went, even though he did not know where he was going. By faith he made his home in the promised land like a stranger in a foreign country; he lived in tents, as did Isaac and Jacob, who were heirs with him of the same promise. For he was looking forward to the city with foundations, whose architect and builder is God. And by faith even Sarah, who was past childbearing age, was enabled to bear children because she considered Him faithful who had made the promise. And so from this one man, and he as good as dead, came descendants as numerous as the stars in the sky and as countless as the sand on the seashore.

All these people were still living by faith when they died. They did not receive the things promised; they only saw them and welcomed them from a distance, admitting that they were foreigners and strangers on earth. People who say such things show that they are looking for a country of their own. If they had been thinking of the country they had left, they would have had opportunity to return. Instead, they were longing for a better country - a heavenly one. Therefore God is not ashamed to be called their God, for He has prepared a city for them.

By faith Abraham, when God tested him, offered Isaac as a sacrifice. He who had embraced the promises was about to sacrifice his one and only son, even though God had said to him, "It is through Isaac that your offspring will be reckoned." Abraham reasoned that God could even raise the dead, and so in a manner of speaking he did receive Isaac back from death.

By faith Isaac blessed Jacob and Esau in regard to their future.

By faith Jacob, when he was dying, blessed each of Joseph's sons, and worshiped as he leaned on the top of his staff.

By faith Joseph, when his end was near, spoke about the exodus of the Israelites from Egypt and gave instructions concerning the burial of his bones.

By faith Moses' parents hid him for three months after he was born, because they saw he was no ordinary child, and they were not afraid of the king's edict.

By faith Moses, when he had grown up, refused to be known as the son of Pharaoh's daughter. He chose to be mistreated along with the people of God rather than to enjoy the fleeting pleasures of sin. He regarded disgrace for the sake of Christ as of greater value than the treasures of Egypt, because he was looking ahead to his reward. By faith he left Egypt, not fearing the king's anger; he persevered because he saw him who is invisible. By faith he kept the Passover and the application of blood, so that the destroyer of the firstborn would not touch the firstborn of Israel.

By faith the people passed through the Red Sea as on dry land; but when the Egyptians tried to do so, they were drowned.

By faith the walls of Jericho fell, after the army had
marched around them for seven days.

By faith the prostitute Rahab, because she welcomed
the spies, was not killed with those who were disobedient.

And what more shall I say? I do not have time to tell
about Gideon, Barak, Samson and Jephthah, about David
and Samuel and the prophets, who through faith
conquered kingdoms, administered justice, and gained
what was promised; who shut the mouths of lions,
quenched the fury of the flames, and escaped the edge of
the sword; whose weakness was turned to strength; and
who became powerful in battle and routed foreign armies.
Women received back their dead, raised to life again.
There were others who were tortured, refusing to be
released so that they might gain an even better resurrection. Some faced jeers and flogging, and even chains and
imprisonment. They were put to death by stoning; they
were sawed in two; they were killed by the sword. They
went about in sheepskins and goatskins, destitute, perse-
cuted and mistreated - the world was not worthy of them.
They wandered in deserts and mountains, living in caves
and in holes in the ground.

These were all commended for their faith, yet none of
them received what had been promised, since God had
planned something better for us so that only together with
us would they be made perfect. (NIV)

PRAYER FOCUS:
Thank You for the example of these men and women

who exhibited such strong faith. Show me how I can emulate each one that I might also be commended for my faith.

Elul Day 11

As we saw yesterday, faith can be both sacrificial and spiritual, but it can also be very practical. We can show our faith in many outward ways to a lost and dying world. Some examples are: acts of service, intercessory prayer for others, or the way we conduct ourselves within various organizations. (Even within the church!) We can even exhibit faith in the way we manage our households and our time. Living as a person of faith can and should be intertwined with every aspect of life.

SCRIPTURE:

James 1: 27

Religion that God our Father accepts as pure and faultless is this: to look after orphans and widows in their distress and to keep oneself from being polluted by the world. (NIV)

LUKE 10: 30 - 37

In reply Jesus said: "A man was going down from Jerusalem to Jericho, when he was attacked by robbers. They stripped him of his clothes, beat him and went away, leaving him half dead. A priest happened to be going down the same road, and when he saw the man, he passed by on the other side. So too, a Levite, when he came to the place and saw him, passed by on the other side. But a Samaritan, as he traveled, came where the man was; and when he saw him, he took pity on him. He went to him and bandaged his wounds, pouring on oil and wine. Then he put the man on his own donkey, brought him to an inn and took care of him. The next day he took out two denarii and gave them to the innkeeper. 'Look after him,' he said, 'and when I return, I will reimburse you for any extra expense you may have.'

"Which of these three do you think was a neighbour to the man who fell into the hands of robbers?"

The expert in the law replied, "The one who had mercy on him."

Jesus told him, "Go and do likewise." (NIV)

PRAYER FOCUS:

Help me to look for opportunities to show my faith in practical ways. May I always be a person of integrity in every place that I find myself, putting others first.

Elul Day 12

The familiar phrase, "I am my beloved's and my beloved is mine," from Song of Solomon 6:3 is actually an acrostic that spells out the word ELUL! This month it is time to come out of mourning after the low points of the past two months and regain a new level of intimacy with God. When we submit both our actions and our emotions to God, He can draw even nearer to us.

SCRIPTURE:

Psalm 37

Do not fret because of those who are evil
or be envious of those who do wrong;
for like the grass they will soon wither,
like green plants they will soon die away.
Trust in the Lord and do good;
dwell in the land and enjoy safe pasture.
Take delight in the Lord,
and He will give you the desires of your heart.
Commit your way to the Lord;
trust in Him and He will do this:
He will make your righteous reward
shine like the dawn,
your vindication like the noonday sun.
Be still before the Lord
and wait patiently for Him;
do not fret when people succeed in their ways,
when they carry out their wicked schemes.
Refrain from anger and turn from wrath;
do not fret - it leads only to evil.

For those who are evil will be destroyed,
but those who hope in the Lord will inherit the land.
A little while, and the wicked will be no more;
though you look for them, they will not be found.
But the meek will inherit the land
and enjoy peace and prosperity.
The wicked plot against the righteous
and gnash their teeth at them;
but the Lord laughs at the wicked,
for He knows their day is coming.
The wicked draw the sword
and bend the bow
to bring down the poor and needy,
to slay those whose ways are upright.
But their swords will pierce their own hearts,
and their bows will be broken.
Better the little that the righteous have
than the wealth of many wicked;
for the power of the wicked will be broken,
but the Lord upholds the righteous.
The blameless spend their days under the Lord's care,
and their inheritance will endure forever.
In times of disaster they will not wither;
in days of famine they will enjoy plenty.
But the wicked will perish:
Though the Lord's enemies
are like the flowers of the field,
they will be consumed, they will go up in smoke.
The wicked borrow and do not repay,
but the righteous give generously;
those the Lord blesses will inherit the land,

but those He curses will be destroyed.
The Lord makes firm the steps
of the one who delights in Him;
though he may stumble, he will not fall,
for the Lord upholds him with His hand.
I was young and now I am old,
yet I have never seen the righteous forsaken
or their children begging bread.
They are always generous and lend freely;
their children will be a blessing.
Turn from evil and do good;
then you will dwell in the land forever.
For the Lord loves the just
and will not forsake His faithful ones.
Wrongdoers will be completely destroyed;
the offspring of the wicked will perish.
The righteous will inherit the land
and dwell in it forever.
The mouths of the righteous utter wisdom,
and their tongues speak what is just.
The law of their God is in their hearts;
their feet do not slip.
The wicked lie in wait for the righteous,
intent on putting them to death;
but the Lord will not leave them
in the power of the wicked
or let them be condemned when brought to trial.
Hope in the Lord and keep his way.
He will exalt you to inherit the land;
when the wicked are destroyed, you will see it.
I have seen a wicked and ruthless man

flourishing like a luxuriant native tree,
but he soon passed away and was no more;
though I looked for him, he could not be found.
Consider the blameless, observe the upright;
a future awaits those who seek peace.
But all sinners will be destroyed;
there will be no future for the wicked.
The salvation of the righteous comes from the Lord;
He is their stronghold in time of trouble.
The Lord helps them and delivers them;
He delivers them from the wicked and saves them,
because they take refuge in Him. (NIV)

PRAYER FOCUS:

Thank You that I am beloved by You, Lord, and that You desire goodness and plenty for me. Forgive me for the times I have been impatient for You to exact revenge or to do things my way. Instead, I trust in Your sovereignty, for Your love is everlasting and You desire that I embrace You and Your ways. Show me how I can come closer to You. Enable me to surrender all so that I may live more intimately in Your care.

Elul Day 13

In keeping with the theme of repentance, mercy, and forgiveness, this month follows the two great sins of the Israelites: worshiping the golden calf in Tammuz and the spies disbelief in Av. Yet God was merciful and still wanted a relationship with His people. As we saw earlier, Moses ascended Mount Sinai a second time to receive the second set of tablets. God continues to give us second chances, too, no matter what we have done or will do in the future, and no matter how tired or discouraged we may be.

Scripture:

Isaiah 40: 28 - 31
Do you not know? Have you not heard?
The Everlasting God, the Lord,
the Creator of the ends of the earth
Does not become weary or tired.
His understanding is inscrutable.
He gives strength to the weary,
And to him who lacks might He increases power.
Though youths grow weary and tired,
And vigorous young men stumble badly,
Yet those who wait for the Lord
Will gain new strength;
They will mount up with wings like eagles,
They will run and not get tired,
They will walk and not become weary.
(NASB)

. . .

PRAYER FOCUS:

Praise You that You are a God of second chances. Even more than this, You continue to show Your mercy immeasurable times. Forgive me, for I am a sinner, and I realize that I am deserving of death, but You have chosen to make me clean and worthy because of the shed blood of Jesus. Help me to leave the past in the past and to move forward victoriously, with You as my guide. Give me new strength for each day.

Elul Day 14

Elul is a month of preparation for the holiest month coming next—Tishrei. It is during Tishrei that the fall feasts take place, including the Day of Atonement followed by the Feast of Booths. God wants us to begin preparing our hearts through recognition of our sin followed by repentance, so that we can come into His presence with clean hearts.

SCRIPTURE:

1 Samuel 7: 3

Then Samuel spoke to all the house of Israel, saying, "If you return to the Lord with all your heart, remove the foreign gods and the Ashtaroth from among you and direct your hearts to the Lord and serve Him alone; and He will deliver you from the hand of the Philistines." (NASB)

PSALM 51:10

Create in me a clean heart, O God, and renew a right spirit within me. (ESV)

1 SAMUEL 15:22

But Samuel replied: "Does the Lord delight in burnt offerings and sacrifices as much as in obeying the Lord? To obey is better than sacrifice, and to heed is better than the fat of rams. (NIV)

.   .   .

PRAYER FOCUS:

Show me what things have become idols in my life, Lord, so that I may remove them and repent. I pledge to direct my heart toward You and You alone, God my Saviour and my rock. Deliver me from the hands of my enemies and prepare me for a divine encounter with You in the coming month.

Elul Day 15

Some Jewish traditions call this month the 'eye of the needle'. God desires to meet with us, but it is up to us to open up to Him, even in a small way, so that He may come in. It is like a minute but specific entry point—a window of opportunity—for God to do something miraculous. I love the way this fits so well with Jesus' parable about the camel fitting through the eye of a needle, because nothing is impossible with God! Carrying the analogy further, He is in charge of sewing together the tapestry of our lives. We can fully trust Him with every aspect of it.

SCRIPTURE:

Mark 10: 23 - 27

And Jesus looked around and said to his disciples, "How difficult it will be for those who have wealth to enter the kingdom of God!" And the disciples were amazed at His words. But Jesus said to them again, "Children, how difficult it is to enter the kingdom of God! It is easier for a camel to go through the eye of a needle than for a rich person to enter the kingdom of God." And they were exceedingly astonished, and said to Him, "Then who can be saved?" Jesus looked at them and said, "With man it is impossible, but not with God. For all things are possible with God." (ESV)

MARK 9: 17 - 23

A man in the crowd answered, "Teacher, I brought you my son, who is possessed by a spirit that has robbed him of speech. Whenever it seizes him, it throws him to the ground. He foams at the mouth, gnashes his teeth and becomes rigid. I asked your disciples to drive out the spirit, but they could not."

"You unbelieving generation," Jesus replied, "how long shall I stay with you? How long shall I put up with you? Bring the boy to me."

So they brought him. When the spirit saw Jesus, it immediately threw the boy into a convulsion. He fell to the ground and rolled around, foaming at the mouth.

Jesus asked the boy's father, "How long has he been like this?"

"From childhood," he answered. "It has often thrown him into fire or water to kill him. But if you can do anything, take pity on us and help us."

" 'If you can'?" said Jesus. "Everything is possible for one who believes." (NIV)

PRAYER FOCUS:

What part of my life have I not yet put completely in Your hands, Lord? Help me to commit even the smallest things to You, for these small things could be a window of opportunity that You are going to open up. I know that Your plans for me are good. May Your Holy Spirit enter and invade my soul, rushing in with power from on high. Forgive my unbelief. Forgive me for becoming anxious over the details of this life. Instead, help me to surrender as I commit all to You.

Elul Day 16

Everyone experiences challenges in life. Perhaps the past few months have been difficult, even laced with mourning or grief. Certainly this was the case for the children of Israel, as we have seen. While there is an appropriate season for mourning, it isn't healthy to stay in grief mode forever. Embrace the growth that has occurred because of the losses of the past, but move on. Naomi and Ruth are fine examples of this principle in action. They had both been widowed. They had lost everything. But at the appropriate time, Naomi instructed Ruth to change her clothes and take steps to move forward in her life. We should also make a redemptive shift after an appropriate season, keeping our eyes on Jesus, not on our past.

SCRIPTURE:

Ruth 3: 1 - 5

Then Naomi her mother-in-law said to her, "My daughter, should I not seek rest for you, that it may be well with you? Is not Boaz our relative, with whose young women you were? See, he is winnowing barley tonight at the threshing floor. Wash therefore and anoint yourself, and put on your cloak and go down to the threshing floor, but do not make yourself known to the man until he has finished eating and drinking. But when he lies down, observe the place where he lies. Then go and uncover his feet and lie down, and he will tell you what to do." And she replied, "All that you say I will do." (ESV)

·   ·   ·

Philippians 3: 7 - 14

But whatever were gains to me I now consider loss for the sake of Christ. What is more, I consider everything a loss because of the surpassing worth of knowing Christ Jesus my Lord, for whose sake I have lost all things. I consider them garbage, that I may gain Christ and be found in Him, not having a righteousness of my own that comes from the law, but that which is through faith in Christ - the righteousness that comes from God on the basis of faith. I want to know Christ - yes, to know the power of His resurrection and participation in His sufferings, becoming like Him in His death, and so, somehow, attaining to the resurrection from the dead.

Not that I have already obtained all this, or have already arrived at my goal, but I press on to take hold of that for which Christ Jesus took hold of me. Brothers and sisters, I do not consider myself yet to have taken hold of it. But one thing I do: Forgetting what is behind and straining toward what is ahead, I press on toward the goal to win the prize for which God has called me heavenward in Christ Jesus. (NIV)

Prayer focus:

A shift has been happening already in my life and in the lives of my loved ones. I claim the promises of God in Jesus name and purposely make a redemptive shift into greater surrender to You. May I live like the child of the King that I am. I claim all Your promises—for healing, provision, and victory, and I walk out the destiny that You have already preordained for me. I pray that You would show me how to bring my entire life into alignment with You, leaving the past behind and focusing solely on You.

Elul Day 17

Elul is the month associated with Gad, who was Jacob's seventh son born to Leah's maid, Zilpah. When he was born, Leah cried, "Fortunate!" which led to his name which means, "Good fortune." She was happy and embraced what she saw as good fortune because she was responsible for yet another son for her husband—even though it was by another woman. Leah saw it as a reward. So too, there will be a time of reward for us in our lives if we have been faithful to the Lord. Sometimes people feel awkward about desiring or even accepting their just reward. However, God desires to give us good gifts and it is okay to embrace the reward that is due.

Scripture:

Genesis 30: 9 - 11

When Leah saw that she had stopped having children, she took her servant Zilpah and gave her to Jacob as a wife. Leah's servant Zilpah bore Jacob a son. Then Leah said, "What good fortune!" So she named him Gad.

(NIV)

Proverbs 31: 30 - 31

Charm is deceptive, and beauty does not last; but a woman who fears the Lord will be greatly praised. Reward her for all she has done. Let her deeds publicly declare her praise. (NLT)

· · ·

Psalm 19

    The heavens declare the glory of God;
    the skies proclaim the work of His hands.
    Day after day they pour forth speech;
    night after night they reveal knowledge.
    They have no speech, they use no words;
    no sound is heard from them.
    Yet their voice goes out into all the earth,
    their words to the ends of the world.
    In the heavens God has pitched a tent for the sun.
    It is like a bridegroom coming out of his chamber,
    like a champion rejoicing to run his course.
    It rises at one end of the heavens
    and makes its circuit to the other;
    nothing is deprived of its warmth.
    The law of the Lord is perfect,
    refreshing the soul.
    The statutes of the Lord are trustworthy,
    making wise the simple.
    The precepts of the Lord are right,
    giving joy to the heart.
    The commands of the Lord are radiant,
    giving light to the eyes.
    The fear of the Lord is pure,
    enduring forever.
    The decrees of the Lord are firm,
    and all of them are righteous.
    They are more precious than gold,
    than much pure gold;
    they are sweeter than honey,
    than honey from the honeycomb.

By them your servant is warned;
in keeping them there is great reward.
But who can discern their own errors?
Forgive my hidden faults.
Keep your servant also from willful sins;
may they not rule over me.
Then I will be blameless,
innocent of great transgression.
May these words of my mouth
and this meditation of my heart
be pleasing in your sight,
Lord, my Rock and my Redeemer. (NIV)

PRAYER FOCUS:

I embrace the good things that You have given me already, Lord, and open myself up to what you have in store for my future. I recognize that all things come from You; that You made the heavens and the earth and that You are sovereign. Help me to be like the woman in Proverbs, serving You diligently with my whole heart. May I never get puffed up or full of pride because of what You are doing. Instead, help me to focus on Your Word, for in knowing You there is great reward.

Elul Day 18

This is a wonderful month to activate the peace of God that passes all understanding. It is time to rest in Him and regroup in spirit, soul and body.

SCRIPTURE:

Philippians 4: 4 - 7

Rejoice in the Lord always; again I will say, rejoice. Let your reasonableness be known to everyone. The Lord is at hand; do not be anxious about anything, but in everything by prayer and supplication with thanksgiving let your requests be made known to God. And the peace of God, which surpasses all understanding, will guard your hearts and your minds in Christ Jesus. (ESV)

COLOSSIANS 3: 15

Let the peace of Christ rule in your hearts, since as members of one body you were called to peace. And be thankful. (NIV)

PSALM 37: 7a

Be still before the Lord and wait patiently for him. (ESV)

HEBREWS 4: 1   11

Therefore, since the promise of entering His rest still

stands, let us be careful that none of you be found to have fallen short of it. For we also have had the good news proclaimed to us, just as they did; but the message they heard was of no value to them, because they did not share the faith of those who obeyed. Now we who have believed enter that rest, just as God has said,

"So I declared on oath in my anger, 'They shall never enter My rest.' "

And yet His works have been finished since the creation of the world. For somewhere He has spoken about the seventh day in these words: "On the seventh day God rested from all His works." And again in the passage above He says, "They shall never enter My rest."

Therefore since it still remains for some to enter that rest, and since those who formerly had the good news proclaimed to them did not go in because of their disobedience, God again set a certain day, calling it "Today." This He did when a long time later He spoke through David, as in the passage already quoted:

"Today, if you hear His voice, do not harden your hearts."

For if Joshua had given them rest, God would not have spoken later about another day. There remains, then, a Sabbath-rest for the people of God; for anyone who enters God's rest also rests from their works, just as God did from His. Let us, therefore, make every effort to enter that rest, so that no one will perish by following their example of disobedience. (NIV)

.   .   .

PRAYER FOCUS:

Let Your peace reign in my mind, heart and body. I release everything that causes me stress and anxiety, believing that You are in control. I seek Your rest, Lord, so that I can regroup and prepare myself for the next stage of the coming year—as well as the rest of my life.

Elul Day 19

Jacob's blessing over his sons included an interesting 'turn around' for Gad. Even though Gad would suffer some form of loss, he would also triumph in the end. This is a wonderful promise for us as well. Even though we may suffer attack, in the end we know who wins—God! When we put our faith in Him we are always on the winning side.

SCRIPTURE:

Genesis 49: 19

Gad will be attacked by a band of raiders, but he will attack them at their heels. (NIV)

COLOSSIANS 2: 6 - 13

So then, just as you received Christ Jesus as Lord, continue to live your lives in Him, rooted and built up in Him, strengthened in the faith as you were taught, and overflowing with thankfulness.

See to it that no one takes you captive through hollow and deceptive philosophy, which depends on human tradition and the elemental spiritual forces of this world rather than on Christ.

For in Christ all the fullness of the Deity lives in bodily form, and in Christ you have been brought to fullness. He is the head over every power and authority. In Him you were also circumcised with a circumcision not performed by human hands. Your whole self ruled by the flesh was put off when you were circumcised by Christ, having been buried with Him in baptism, in which you were also raised with Him through your faith in the working of God, who raised Him from the dead.

When you were dead in your sins and in the uncircumcision of your flesh, God made you alive with Christ. He forgave us all our sins, having canceled the charge of our legal indebtedness, which stood against us and condemned us; He has taken it away, nailing it to the cross. And having disarmed the powers and authorities, He made a public spectacle of them, triumphing over them by the cross. (NIV)

REVELATION 21: 1 - 4

Then I saw a new heaven and a new earth, for the first heaven and the first earth had passed away, and the sea was no more. And I saw the holy city, new Jerusalem, coming down out of heaven from God, prepared as a bride adorned for her husband. And I heard a loud voice from the throne saying, "Behold, the dwelling place of God is with man. He will dwell with them, and they will be His people, and God himself will be with them as their God. He will wipe away every tear from their eyes, and death shall be no more, neither shall there be mourning, nor crying, nor pain anymore, for the former things have passed away." (ESV)

PRAYER FOCUS:

Hallelujah and praise to You, Lord, for You win the war! Despite the devil's attempts, we know beyond a shadow of a doubt that the final victory is Yours. Thank

You that You disarmed every demon and every devil; every scheme of the enemy must let go of its grip on me and on my household, for You paid the price and those forces no longer have any legal authority over my life or the lives of my loved ones. You took the pain and suffering and sin upon Your own shoulders, and even though it may sometimes look like the enemy has won, we know the truth—You are victorious! I embrace this principle in my own life. Despite setbacks or difficulties, I know that victory is ultimately mine because I am in You, no matter how it may look at any given moment. I praise You now, for You are worthy of all praise.

Elul Day 20

Moses' blessing over the tribe of Gad contains some powerful imagery. Gad is likened to a lion who can overpower any who come against him. We are told that Satan comes like a roaring lion seeking whom he may devour, but the Lord Jesus is the lion of Judah, able to totally overpower and defeat any other power on earth—or out of it! Some of the wording of Moses' blessing mirror the small but effective prayer prayed by Jabez in the book of 1 Chronicles. While we never want to use such a prayer as some kind of mantra or magic formula, it has merit when prayed with sincerity and conviction.

SCRIPTURE:

Deuteronomy 33: 20 (Moses' blessing)
And of Gad he said,
"Blessed be he who enlarges Gad!
Gad crouches like a lion;
he tears off arm and scalp. (ESV)

REVELATION 5: 5a
And one of the elders said to me, "Weep no more; behold, the Lion of the tribe of Judah, the Root of David, has conquered..." (ESV)

1 CHRONICLES 4:10
Jabez called upon the God of Israel, saying, "Oh that you would bless me and enlarge my border, and that Your

hand might be with me, and that You would keep me from harm so that it might not bring me pain!" And God granted what he asked. (ESV)

PRAYER FOCUS:

Lord, bless me indeed, as I align myself with You and Your Word. Enlarge my territory, even as Your servant Jabez prayed, so that I might be more effective for You. May Your hand continue to guide me in all Your ways, and keep me from evil so that Your great name would never be maligned. I recognize that the enemy is out to sabotage me and my life, but I pray for Your protection and believe that You are stronger—that You, the Lion of Judah, will over-power all those that would come against me.

Elul Day 21

Moses' blessing over the tribe of Gad didn't end with a comparison to a lion. In the second part of the blessing, we see some commendable character traits like commitment to their word, strength, leadership, and justice. Prophetically, we see evidence of this blessing when the tribe of Gad helped the rest of Israel secure their inheritance, even though they had already received theirs on the other side of the Jordan River. They could have said, "We've already chosen our land and don't want to risk our lives to help the rest of you." Instead, they fulfilled their promise to Joshua and did not return to their own inheritance until after their brothers had been looked after.

SCRIPTURE:

Deuteronomy 33: 21 (part two of Moses' blessing)
He chose the best of the land for himself,
for there a commander's portion was reserved;
and he came with the heads of the people,
with Israel he executed the justice of the Lord,
and his judgments for Israel. (ESV)

NUMBERS 32: 28 - 32

So Moses gave command concerning them to Eleazar the priest and to Joshua the son of Nun and to the heads of the fathers' houses of the tribes of the people of Israel. And Moses said to them, "If the people of Gad and the people of Reuben, every man who is armed to battle before the Lord, will pass with you over the Jordan and the land shall be subdued before you, then you shall give them the land of Gilead for a possession. However, if they will not pass over with you armed, they shall have possessions among you in the land of Canaan." And the people of Gad and the people of Reuben answered, "What the Lord has said to your servants, we will do. We will pass over armed before the Lord into the land of Canaan, and the possession of our inheritance shall remain with us beyond the Jordan." (ESV)

JOSHUA 4: 12

The men of Reuben, Gad and the half-tribe of Manasseh crossed over, ready for battle, in front of the Israelites, as Moses had directed them. (NIV)

PRAYER FOCUS:

Help me to be a person of my word, exhibiting strength of character, leadership in the things of You, and a willingness to uphold justice for Your kingdom. I take hold of the inheritance You have given me, understanding that with great reward, also comes a price—full service to You in any and every situation You call me to.

Elul Day 22

As we saw in the month of Tammuz, the people of
Gad, along with their brothers the Reubenites and the half
tribe of Manasseh, claimed their inheritance on the east
side of the Jordan, but still helped the rest of the tribes in
the conquest of Canaan. Even though they were faithful in
honouring their commitments, a huge misunderstanding
arose after they returned to their own land, and they were
almost forced into a war with the very people they had just
helped. Misunderstandings can occur in the blink of an
eye, even between friends and believers. When this
happens, it is up to us to examine our own motives and
then make every effort to diffuse the situation in order to
maintain harmony and thus honour God.

Scripture:

Joshua 22: 1 - 5; 9 - 12; 21 - 28

Then Joshua summoned the Reubenites, the Gadites
and the half-tribe of Manasseh and said to them, "You
have done all that Moses the servant of the Lord commanded, and you have obeyed me in everything I
commanded. For a long time now - to this very day - you
have not deserted your fellow Israelites but have carried
out the mission the Lord your God gave you. Now that
the Lord your God has given them rest as He promised,
return to your homes in the land that Moses the servant of
the Lord gave you on the other side of the Jordan. But be
very careful to keep the commandment and the law that
Moses the servant of the Lord gave you: to love
the Lord your God, to walk in obedience to Him, to keep

His commands, to hold fast to Him and to serve Him with all your heart and with all your soul.".....

So the Reubenites, the Gadites and the half-tribe of Manasseh left the Israelites at Shiloh in Canaan to return to Gilead, their own land, which they had acquired in accordance with the command of the Lord through Moses.

When they came to Geliloth near the Jordan in the land of Canaan, the Reubenites, the Gadites and the half-tribe of Manasseh built an imposing altar there by the Jordan. And when the Israelites heard that they had built the altar on the border of Canaan at Geliloth near the Jordan on the Israelite side, the whole assembly of Israel gathered at Shiloh to go to war against them...

Then Reuben, Gad and the half-tribe of Manasseh replied to the heads of the clans of Israel: "The Mighty One, God, the Lord! The Mighty One, God, the Lord! He knows! And let Israel know! If this has been in rebellion or disobedience to the Lord, do not spare us this day. If we have built our own altar to turn away from the Lord and to offer burnt offerings and grain offerings, or to sacrifice fellowship offerings on it, may the Lord Himself call us to account.

"No! We did it for fear that some day your descendants might say to ours, 'What do you have to do with the Lord, the God of Israel? The Lord has made the Jordan a boundary between us and you - you Reubenites and Gadites! You have no share in the Lord.' So your descendants might cause ours to stop fearing the Lord.

"That is why we said, 'Let us get ready and build an altar - but not for burnt offerings or sacrifices.' On the contrary, it is to be a witness between us and you and the generations that follow, that we will worship the Lord at His sanctuary with our burnt offerings, sacrifices and fellowship offerings. Then in the future your descendants will not be able to say to ours, 'You have no share in the Lord.'

"And we said, 'If they ever say this to us, or to our descendants, we will answer: Look at the replica of the Lord's altar, which our ancestors built, not for burnt offerings and sacrifices, but as a witness between us and you.' (NIV)

PRAYER FOCUS:

I pray that You would shine a spotlight on my own motives in every situation, but especially when it comes to my relationships. I know that Satan would like nothing better than to cause offences and to create a rift between friends, family, and fellow believers, but in Your mercy, show me how I can make things right, first and foremost by examining my own heart. Forgive me for when pride or arrogance get in the way, and help me to humble myself before those I come in contact with so that unity may be maintained.

Elul Day 23

The tribe of Gad were valiant men skilled in battle, and as the account from Chronicles states, they relied on the Lord for their strength. Even so, they eventually turned away from God to idols and were sent into exile. This is a sobering lesson for us not to become arrogant or comfortable in our faith, lest we stray from relying on God.

SCRIPTURE:

1 Chronicles 5: 16 - 22, and 26

The Gadites lived in Gilead, in Bashan and its outlying villages, and on all the pasturelands of Sharon as far as they extended. All these were entered in the genealogical records during the reigns of Jotham king of Judah and Jeroboam king of Israel. The Reubenites, the Gadites and the half-tribe of Manasseh had 44,760 men ready for military service - able-bodied men who could handle shield and sword, who could use a bow, and who were trained for battle. They waged war against the Hagrites, Jetur, Naphish and Nodab. They were helped in fighting them, and God delivered the Hagrites and all their allies into their hands, because they cried out to Him during the battle. He answered their prayers, because they trusted in Him. They seized the livestock of the Hagrites - fifty thousand camels, two hundred fifty thousand sheep and two thousand donkeys. They also took one hundred thousand people captive, and many others fell slain, because the battle was God's. And they occupied the land until the exile...

So the God of Israel stirred up the spirit of Pul king of

Assyria (that is, Tiglath-Pileser king of Assyria), who took the Reubenites, the Gadites and the half-tribe of Manasseh into exile. (NIV)

PRAYER FOCUS:

Lord, help me to ever keep my focus and reliance on You. May I not become arrogant or complacent in my faith, but help me to constantly look to You for strength in all of life's battles.

Elul Day 24

In his prophetic vision, Ezekiel places Gad's inheritance next to Zebulun. He also specifies a western gate for their use in the new Jerusalem along with Asher and Naphtali. These arrangements mark a change in the order of the camp from Moses' day. Although we don't know exactly why this would be, we can trust that God never does anything by accident. He always has a design and purpose and it is up to us to be alert, should He ask us to shift our own position in order to fulfill His mandate.

SCRIPTURE:

Ezekiel 48: 27 - 29

"Beside the border of Zebulun, from the east side to the west side, Gad, one portion. And beside the border of Gad, at the south side toward the south, the border shall be from Tamar to the waters of Meribath-kadesh, to the brook of Egypt, to the Great Sea. This is the land which you shall divide by lot to the tribes of Israel for an inheritance, and these are their several portions," declares the Lord God.

(NASB)

EZEKIEL 38: 34

On the west side, 4,500 cubits, shall be three gates: the gate of Gad, one; the gate of Asher, one; the gate of Naphtali, one. (NASB)

. . .

ISAIAH 55: 9

As the heavens are higher than the earth, so are My ways higher than your ways and My thoughts than your thoughts. (NIV)

PSALM 113: 5

Who is like the Lord our God, Who is enthroned on high? (NIV)

JOB 38: 4 - 7

Where were you when I laid the earth's foundation?
Tell me, if you understand.
Who marked off its dimensions?
Surely you know!
Who stretched a measuring line across it?
On what were its footings set,
or who laid its cornerstone -
while the morning stars sang together
and all the angels shouted for joy? (NIV)

PRAYER FOCUS:

I humbly bow before Your throne, recognizing that You are sovereign over all the earth. Forgive me for questioning Your ways when I don't understand them. I am insignificant in the grand scheme of history, yet You care for me as one of Your own. This is such a great mystery, but one for which I am grateful. Help me to always surrender to Your will and Your ways in every situation, both good and what I perceive to be 'bad', trusting that Your plans are always righteous.

Elul Day 25

In today's world, it is easy to feel overwhelmed by the many tasks that keep vying for our time. Work, church, family, home and many other responsibilities and obligations can make us feel like we are spinning our wheels. However, as we surrender our daily activities to God, complex systems can become manageable as He shows us how to put things together. Nothing is too complicated for the Creator of the universe!

SCRIPTURE:

Luke 3: 5

Every valley shall be filled in, every mountain and hill made low. The crooked roads shall become straight, the rough ways smooth. (NIV)

ISAIAH 43: 1 - 7

But now thus says the Lord,
He who created you, O Jacob,
He who formed you, O Israel:
"Fear not, for I have redeemed you;
I have called you by name, you are Mine.
When you pass through the waters, I will be with you;
and through the rivers, they shall not overwhelm you;
when you walk through fire you shall not be burned,
and the flame shall not consume you.
For I am the Lord your God,
the Holy One of Israel, your Saviour.

I give Egypt as your ransom,
Cush and Seba in exchange for you.
Because you are precious in My eyes, and honoured,
and I love you, I give men in return for you,
peoples in exchange for your life.
Fear not, for I am with you;
I will bring your offspring from the east,
and from the west I will gather you.
I will say to the north, "Give up," and to the south,
"Do not withhold; bring my sons from afar
and my daughters from the end of the earth,
everyone who is called by My name,
whom I created for My glory,
whom I formed and made." (ESV)

JEREMIAH 32: 17

Ah Lord God! Behold, You have made the heavens and the earth by Your great power and by Your outstretched arm! Nothing is too difficult for You. (NASB)

PRAYER FOCUS:

I pray that all the complexities of modern life, including all of my projects and my 'to-do' lists, would be distilled down as I focus on You. I pray for divine insight in my day-to-day life that I would be able to serve You without stress; that my life would become manageable as I surrender everything to You. Reveal what things I need to let go of and which things I need to focus on differently. I trust that You can bring order from chaos in my life and the lives of those around me. Bring my life into alignment with You so that I may serve You better and be an example of Your Holy Spirit living in me.

Elul Day 26

We can continue to look for windows of opportunity, even in the wilderness. God has not forsaken or abandoned us, no matter the outward circumstances. The blessing cycle of God has not changed and it is up to us to believe in God's goodness without wavering, for He doesn't change.

SCRIPTURE:

Philippians 1: 12 - 14

Now I want you to know, brothers and sisters, that what has happened to me has actually served to advance the gospel. As a result, it has become clear throughout the whole palace guard and to everyone else that I am in chains for Christ. And because of my chains, most of the brothers and sisters have become confident in the Lord and dare all the more to proclaim the gospel without fear. (NIV)

NUMBERS 23: 19

God is not human, that He should lie, not a human being, that He should change His mind. Does He speak and then not act? Does He promise and not fulfill? (NIV)

ISAIAH 43: 18 - 19

Do not call to mind the former things, or ponder things of the past. "Behold, I will do something new, now it will spring forth; will you not be aware of it? I will even

make a roadway in the wilderness, rivers in the desert.
(NASB)

I CORINTHIANS 9: 24

Do you not know that in a race all the runners run, but
only one gets the prize? Run in such a way as to get the
prize. (NIV)

PRAYER FOCUS:

I thank You that You are the same yesterday, today and
forever. Your promises haven't changed, despite my
circumstances. Help me to keep my eye on the prize, not
get sidetracked by negativity or setbacks. You are doing a
new thing in my life and I embrace it in Jesus name, for
even negative situations can be used for Your glory and
honour.

Elul Day 27

As we saw earlier, Elul is considered a month of nurturing. We all need to be nurtured, but the other side of the question is this: Who am *I* nurturing? Who is under my watch and care? Ponder the relationships that God has put you in, and pray daily for those who are under Your authority, care and mentorship.

SCRIPTURE:

Ephesians 6: 1 - 9

Children, obey your parents in the Lord, for this is right. "Honour your father and mother" (this is the first commandment with a promise), "that it may go well with you and that you may live long in the land." Fathers, do not provoke your children to anger, but bring them up in the discipline and instruction of the Lord. Bondservants, obey your earthly masters with fear and trembling, with a sincere heart, as you would Christ, not by the way of eye-service, as people-pleasers, but as bondservants of Christ, doing the will of God from the heart, rendering service with a good will as to the Lord and not to man, knowing that whatever good anyone does, this he will receive back from the Lord, whether he is a bondservant or is free. Masters, do the same to them, and stop your threatening, knowing that He who is both their Master and yours is in heaven, and that there is no partiality with Him. (ESV)

ROMANS 12: 9 - 13

Let love be genuine. Abhor what is evil; hold fast to

what is good. Love one another with brotherly affection. Out do one another in showing honour. Do not be slothful in zeal, be fervent in spirit, serve the Lord. Rejoice in hope, be patient in tribulation, be constant in prayer. Contribute to the needs of the saints and seek to show hospitality. (ESV)

ROMANS 13: 8 - 10

Owe no one anything, except to love each other, for the one who loves another has fulfilled the law. For the commandments, "You shall not commit adultery, You shall not murder, You shall not steal, You shall not covet," and any other commandment, are summed up in this word: "You shall love your neighbour as yourself." Love does no wrong to a neighbour; therefore love is the fulfilling of the law. (ESV)

PRAYER FOCUS:

Give me a genuine love for others, Lord. Show me how to nurture those that You have put within my sphere of influence. Help me to love others with the kind of love that is straight from You.

Elul Day 28

The month of Elul falls right in the middle of the calendar year. It is like a pivotal point in time as we move in an upward trajectory to the holy days of Tishrei. It is a good opportunity to examine our lives and try to understand how certain situations started so that we can move forward and reach a positive conclusion. God may show us, through various means, (prophetic dreams, visions, words of knowledge, or scripture) the roots of any given situation or problem, enabling us to pray more effectively. This is especially important when dealing with certain bondages, generational curses, or ungodly activity. When we know the root, we can expose it, digging it out as we are directed by the Holy Spirit. Take some time to ask God how you (or a loved one) got into a particular mess, and then ask Him how to get out of it.

Scripture:

Luke 10: 17 - 20

The seventy-two returned with joy and said, "Lord, even the demons submit to us in Your name."

He replied, "I saw Satan fall like lightning from heaven. I have given you authority to trample on snakes and scorpions and to overcome all the power of the enemy; nothing will harm you. However, do not rejoice that the spirits submit to you, but rejoice that your names are written in heaven."

(NIV)

.   .   .

2 Corinthians 13: 5 - 9

Examine yourselves, to see whether you are in the faith. Test yourselves. Or do you not realize this about yourselves, that Jesus Christ is in you? - unless indeed you fail to meet the test! I hope you will find out that we have not failed the test. But we pray to God that you may not do wrong - not that we may appear to have met the test, but that you may do what is right, though we may seem to have failed. For we cannot do anything against the truth, but only for the truth. For we are glad when we are weak and you are strong. Your restoration is what we pray for. (ESV)

Malachi 4: 1

For behold, the day is coming, burning like an oven, when all the arrogant and all evildoers will be stubble. The day that is coming shall set them ablaze, says the Lord of hosts, so that it will leave them neither root nor branch. (ESV)

Prayer focus:

Lord, I pray that this day would be a pivotal point in time—that You would reveal to me the roots of iniquity in my life and any other root or starting point that has led to sin within my family or that has affected those I love. Show me, even by divine means, exactly what I am dealing with and how I should proceed in prayer. I know the battle is Yours and nothing is impossible for You. Show me points in time where curses took root or damage occurred, and then empower me to pray specifically into those situations so that a turning point would take place and victory would be the final outcome.

Elul Day 29

On this last day of Elul, we come to God remembering that we are sanctified by the blood of Jesus Christ our Lord. Peace is ours because He dwells within us. We prepare our hearts for the next month, anticipating a visitation from God through His Holy Spirit, leading to a deeper relationship with Him.

SCRIPTURE:

Psalm 77
I cried out to God for help;
I cried out to God to hear me.
When I was in distress, I sought the Lord;
at night I stretched out untiring hands,
and I would not be comforted.
I remembered You, God, and I groaned;
I meditated, and my spirit grew faint.
You kept my eyes from closing;
I was too troubled to speak.
I thought about the former days,
the years of long ago;
I remembered my songs in the night.
My heart meditated and my spirit asked:
"Will the Lord reject forever?
Will He never show his favour again?
Has His unfailing love vanished forever?
Has His promise failed for all time?
Has God forgotten to be merciful?
Has He in anger withheld His compassion?"
Then I thought, "To this I will appeal:

the years when the Most High
stretched out His right hand.
I will remember the deeds of the Lord;
yes, I will remember Your miracles
of long ago.
I will consider all Your works
and meditate on all Your mighty deeds."
Your ways, God, are holy.
What god is as great as our God?
You are the God who performs miracles;
You display Your power among the peoples.
With Your mighty arm
You redeemed Your people,
the descendants of Jacob and Joseph.
The waters saw You, God,
the waters saw You and writhed;
the very depths were convulsed.
The clouds poured down water,
the heavens resounded with thunder;
Your arrows flashed back and forth.
Your thunder was heard in the whirlwind,
Your lightning lit up the world;
the earth trembled and quaked.
Your path led through the sea,
Your way through the mighty waters,
though Your footprints were not seen.
You led Your people like a flock
by the hand of Moses and Aaron.
(NIV)

. . .

PRAYER FOCUS:

Lord, I prepare my heart today for the coming Feast of Trumpets tomorrow and the other holy days of Tishrei. Cleanse me and open my spiritual eyes that I might see You more clearly. Deepen my love for You and for others. Thank You for all the many blessings You have bestowed on me.

BIBLIOGRAPHY

Gabeli, Giulio Lorefice, *Grafted In*. Winnipeg, Canada; Word Alive Press, 2015

Heidler, Robert D., *The Messianic Church Arising*, Denton, TX; Glory of Zion International, 2006

Peterson, Galen, *Handbook of Bible Festivals*. Cincinnati, Ohio; The Standard Publishing Company, 1997

Pierce, Chuck D., *A Time to Advance*. Denton, TX; Glory of Zion International, 2011

16 Month Biblical Calendar. Upper Tiberias, Israel; Galilee Calendars Ltd, 2017, 2018, 2019, 2020, 2021

http://www.ancient-hebrew.org/alphabet_chart.html

http://www.abarim-publications.com/Hebrew_Alphabet_Meaning.html#.WteJq9PwZok

http://www.hebrew4christians.com/Grammar/Unit_One/Aleph-Bet/Chet/chet.html

SCRIPTURES

Intro

Joel 2: 23 – 25a

Acts 17: 26

Tammuz

Genesis 30: 14 - 16

Genesis 35: 22; 23

Genesis 37: 17 – 22

Genesis 42: 21 - 38

Genesis 49: 1 - 4

Exodus 13: 2 and 12

Exodus 32: 4 – 8

Numbers 2: 10 - 17

Numbers 3: 12

Numbers 13: 1 – 3; 17 – 24

Numbers 14: 6 - 10

Numbers 32: 1 – 7; 16 - 25

Deuteronomy 9: 16

Deuteronomy 11: 26 – 32
Deuteronomy 30: 15 - 19
Deuteronomy 33: 6
Joshua 22: 1 – 6; 10 - 34
Joshua 24: 14 – 15
2 Kings 6: 17
1 Chronicles 5: 1; 26
1 Chronicles 11: 1 – 3; 10; 42
Job 1: 20 – 22
Psalm 8
Psalm 30
Psalm 46
Psalm 118
Psalm 119: 57 – 64
Psalm 121
Proverbs 4: 27
Song of Solomon 5: 2 - 9
Song of Solomon 7: 11 – 13
Isaiah 6: 1 - 8
Isaiah 12: 1 - 2; 3 - 6
Isaiah 59: 17
Isaiah 60: 1 – 4
Lamentations 3: 22 - 33
Jeremiah 31: 13
Ezekiel 1
Ezekiel 2
Ezekiel 3: 17 - 18
Matthew 5: 16; 38 - 42
Matthew 28: 18 – 20
Luke 7: 41 - 47
John 8: 2 - 11

Av

Psalm 139

Psalm 145: 8

Proverbs 3: 11 – 12

Proverbs 10: 4 – 5; 14

Proverbs 15: 8

Proverbs 19: 5

Proverbs 25: 13

Proverbs 26: 1

Isaiah 5: 20 -24

Isaiah 24: 14 – 16

Isaiah 40: 1 - 5

Isaiah 42: 1 – 16

Isaiah 44: 1 – 5

Isaiah 48: 6 - 7

Isaiah 61: 3

Jeremiah 29: 10 - 14

Ezekiel 48: 24; 33

Amos 3: 7 – 8

Zechariah 7: 2 - 10

Micah 6: 6 - 8

Matthew 5: 39

John 2: 18 – 22

John 10: 3 - 5

John 12: 37 – 42

Acts 3: 19

Acts 8: 9 - 24

Romans 3: 23

Romans 4: 7 - 17

Romans 6: 20 - 23

Romans 11; 22 - 32

Romans 12: 19

2 Corinthians 1: 3 - 17

2 Corinthians 5: 17

2 Corinthians 10: 4 – 5

Galatians 5: 1

Galatians 6: 9

1 Thessalonians 2: 11 - 12

1 Timothy 1: 12 – 17; 18 - 19

2 Timothy 4: 2

Hebrews 3: 7 – 19

Hebrews 4: 1 - 2

Hebrews 12: 11; 15

James 1: 9 - 15

James 4: 7

1 Peter 5: 8

Elul

Genesis 17: 19

Genesis 22: 1 – 18

Genesis 25: 21 – 24

Genesis 30: 9 – 11

Genesis 49: 19

Exodus 34: 1 – 9

Numbers 2: 10 – 17

Numbers 23: 19

Numbers 32: 28 - 32

Deuteronomy 33: 20 - 21

Joshua 4: 12

Joshua 22: 1 – 5; 9 – 12; 21 - 28

Ruth 3: 1 - 5

1 Samuel 7: 3

1 Samuel 15: 22

1 Chronicles 4: 10

1 Chronicles 5: 16 – 22; 26

Job 38: 4 - 7

Psalm 19

Psalm 37

Psalm 51: 10

Psalm 77

Psalm 91: 4

Psalm 113: 5

Psalm 119: 73 – 80

Proverbs 14: 26; 33

Proverbs 18: 10

Proverbs 31: 30 - 31

Song of Solomon 6: 3

Isaiah 40: 28 – 31

Isaiah 43: 1 – 7: 18 - 19

Isaiah 55: 9

Ezekiel 38: 27 – 29; 34

Malachi 4: 1

Mark 9: 17 – 23

Mark 10: 23 – 27

Luke 3: 5

Luke 10: 17 20; 30 – 37

Luke 11: 28

John 1: 14

Romans 2: 13 – 16

Romans 12: 9 – 13

Romans 13: 8 - 10

1 Corinthians 9: 24

2 Corinthians 8: 11

2 Corinthians 13: 5 - 9

Ephesians 3: 12

Ephesians 6: 1 - 9

Philippians 1: 12 - 14

Philippians 3: 7 – 14

Philippians 4: 4 – 7

Colossians 3: 13

Hebrews 4: 1 – 11; 16

Hebrews 6: 17

Hebrews 10: 23 - 25

Hebrews 11

James 1: 22; 27

James 2: 14 - 26

James 4: 1

Revelation 5: 5a

Revelation 21: 1 – 4

MORE IN THE SERIES

Get all four seasons of DIVINE APPOINTMENTS: DAILY DEVOTIONALS BASED ON GOD'S CALENDAR wherever good books are sold.

Visit Tracy's website for more titles including other devotional books, fiction and stage plays:
     https://tracykrauss.com

If you enjoyed this book, please consider writing a review online. Reviews help readers find books they'll love and are tremendously helpful for today's authors. Thank you in advance!

Join Tracy's mailing list and get up to date info on all new releases, promos and giveaways when they happen. You'll also get a free book!

ABOUT THE AUTHOR

Tracy Krauss is a multi-published novelist, playwright, and artist with several award winning and best selling novels, stage plays, devotionals and children's books in print. Her work strikes a chord with those looking for thought provoking faith based fiction laced with romance, suspense and humor. She holds a B.Ed from the University of Saskatchewan and has lived in many remote and interesting places in Canada's far north. She and her husband currently reside in beautiful Tumbler Ridge, BC where she continues to pursue all of her creative interests.

"Fiction on the edge – without crossing the line"
https://tracykrauss.com
or contact: tracy@tracykrauss.com